State of the Bible

USA 2025

RESEARCH FROM AMERICAN BIBLE SOCIETY

Prepared by

JEFFERY FULKS, PH.D.

RANDY PETERSEN

JOHN FARQUHAR PLAKE, PH.D.

SANDRA SIGGINS

STATE OF THE BIBLE: USA 2025

© 2025 American Bible Society. All rights reserved.

Final edition (December 2025)

ISBN 978-1-58516-744-9   ABS item 125810 (paperback)
ISBN 978-1-58516-745-6   ABS item 125811 (digital)

Printed in the United States of America.

Unless otherwise noted, Scripture quotations in this publication are from the Good News Translation® *(Today's English Version,* Second Edition) © 1992 American Bible Society. All rights reserved.

AMERICAN BIBLE SOCIETY
101 North Independence Mall East FL8
Philadelphia PA 19106

americanbible.org | **stateofthebible.org**

Order more print copies of this resource at **bibles.com** or call us at 1-800-32-BIBLE.

TABLE OF CONTENTS

PREFACE i

INTRODUCTION: TIME FOR INNOVATION v

CHAPTER 1: THE BIBLE IN AMERICA TODAY 1

CHAPTER 2: THE BIBLE AROUND THE WORLD 21

CHAPTER 3: HUMAN FLOURISHING 45

CHAPTER 4: SELF-CARE AND WELL-BEING 69

CHAPTER 5: CHURCH ENGAGEMENT 91

CHAPTER 6: IDENTITY 111

CHAPTER 7: TRUST 129

CHAPTER 8: LOVE AND GENEROSITY   153

CHAPTER 9:
LOOKING BACK AND LOOKING FORWARD   171

APPENDIX 1: METHODOLOGY   189

APPENDIX 2: DEFINITIONS   193

APPENDIX 3:
PATHWAY OF SCRIPTURE ENGAGEMENT   203

ACKNOWLEDGMENTS   207

TABLE OF CONTENTS

PREFACE   i

INTRODUCTION: TIME FOR INNOVATION   v

CHAPTER 1: THE BIBLE IN AMERICA TODAY   1

CHAPTER 2: THE BIBLE AROUND THE WORLD   21

CHAPTER 3: HUMAN FLOURISHING   45

CHAPTER 4: SELF-CARE AND WELL-BEING   69

CHAPTER 5: CHURCH ENGAGEMENT   91

CHAPTER 6: IDENTITY   111

CHAPTER 7: TRUST   129

CHAPTER 8: LOVE AND GENEROSITY   153

CHAPTER 9:
LOOKING BACK AND LOOKING FORWARD   171

APPENDIX 1: METHODOLOGY   189

APPENDIX 2: DEFINITIONS   193

APPENDIX 3:
PATHWAY OF SCRIPTURE ENGAGEMENT   203

ACKNOWLEDGMENTS   207

PREFACE

JENNIFER HOLLORAN, DSL

American Bible Society

Welcome to the 2025 *State of the Bible* report! Each year, we explore U.S. Bible engagement trends and cultural perceptions across a wide range of demographics. Our goal is not simply to report findings, but to inform, inspire, and encourage the Church to thoughtfully respond to the spiritual realities of our time.

This year, we're excited to include a new global dimension. In partnership with the British and Foreign Bible Society and their recent PATMOS global survey, we share insights into worldwide Bible engagement, broadening our understanding of the opportunity for Bible access and engagement worldwide.

Over the past few years, our research has revealed a concerning decline in U.S. Bible engagement. Yet in 2024, the U.S. saw a resurgence in Bible sales, a signal of renewed interest. The 2025 data suggest that this potential rebound may be taking root, especially among Millennials and men. Meanwhile, engagement among other groups—including Baby Boomers and women—remains steady.

Why this renewed curiosity about the Bible? One possible reason is the Bible's growing presence in public discourse. With such wide access to Scripture in the U.S., many are choosing to look past others' portrayals of the Bible and discover what the Bible actually says for themselves. The Church has a unique opportunity in this moment— to invite seekers into genuine encounters with the living Word of God. As Psalm 34:8 encourages, "Find out for yourself how good the LORD is."

But perhaps there is another factor at work. The 2025 *World Happiness Report*, a study conducted by the University of Oxford, Gallup, and the United Nations, revealed that U.S. happiness has dropped to a record low. In a world where many feel weary, anxious, or unsatisfied, Scripture offers an enduring message of hope. As Isaiah 40:31 reminds us, "But those who trust in the LORD for help will find their strength renewed …"

This year's *State of the Bible* report also explores themes of trust, identity, and church engagement—critical questions in a time when many are asking, *Who am I? Whom can I trust? Where do I belong?* These questions create an opening for Scripture to shape not just individual lives but our relationships and communities.

At American Bible Society, we believe every person is on a journey with God's Word. We want to do our part to equip the Church to respond to cultural shifts with wisdom and compassion, helping people take the next right step with the transforming power of the

Word of God. Together as the body of Christ, we can welcome those who are searching and point them toward the abundant life that comes from loving God and loving others (Matthew 22:37–38).

We hope the 2025 *State of the Bible* serves as a meaningful resource for you, your church, and your ministry as we join in that God-honoring work. ◼

JENNIFER HOLLORAN, DSL

Jennifer Holloran serves as President and CEO at American Bible Society, sharing decades of experience in the global movement to expand Bible access and engagement. Before joining ABS, she served Wycliffe Bible Translators USA for more than 22 years, most recently as Chief Operating Officer. She holds a doctorate in strategic leadership from Regent University as well as a Master of Business Administration with a specialization in human resources from the University of Central Florida. Jennifer and her husband, Tim, live in Philadelphia, PA, with their daughters, Katherine and Penelope.

TIME FOR INNOVATION

JOHN FARQUHAR PLAKE, PH.D.

American Bible Society

S tate of the Bible: USA 2025 is the fifteenth edition of our annual study about Americans' beliefs, attitudes, and behaviors toward the Bible, faith, and the church. Year after year, we've focused on the tremendously positive impact of Bible engagement and on critical opportunities for the gospel in America. Over this decade-and-a-half, our diligent inquiry has helped us better understand and love our neighbors.

In 2025, we document a new moment of opportunity, as more of our neighbors—especially among younger adults and men—are reaching for the Bible, searching its pages, and experiencing God's voice through it. As we look around, we see signs of hope, and we hope for spiritual renewal in our nation.

God is clearly at work in America, and we rejoice in this, but we also recognize the ongoing need for innovation in Bible ministry.

Thankfully, the church has always been innovative, leveraging new technologies to communicate the gospel, exploring language development through Bible translation, and even pioneering the discipline of cultural anthropology to ensure that the Bible isn't merely delivered everywhere but that God's Word has an opportunity to transform all people.

Christians innovate because *culture is always changing.* Our task is to meet the ever-changing challenges of each new generation with the unchanging Word of God. Second, we innovate because *we care deeply about our neighbors.* We know the life-changing power of the Scriptures. Evidence shows that engagement with the Bible and participation in a vibrant Christian community bring health, well-being, and purpose to millions of our neighbors. Because we care for all Americans—indeed for all people—we want all to be transformed by God's Word.

BEYOND THE BOOK

The *State of the Bible* research team has spent 14 years describing opportunities and obstacles to the Bible in America. Now, in our fifteenth year, we are offering more to help ministry leaders put these insights into practice.

State of the Bible: USA 2025 includes several new features. First, we're going multi-modal by adding audio and video components to each chapter. In 2024, we experimented with podcast-style interviews that accompanied some of our key chapters. This year, we plan to release at least one major ***State of the Bible Podcast*** episode per month, in both audio and video formats.

Second, we know that reading long-form reports like this digital and printed book can be daunting for church leaders with busy schedules. This year, we're launching *Insights from State of the Bible*, a series of short videos, focusing on one important finding each week. With an investment of less than two minutes per week, you'll be able to zoom in on a single insight and start a discussion about how to take action in your church or community. This isn't just a way to make our research findings bite-sized, it's an invitation to join us in both conversation and innovation.

Third, we will be preparing a **Church Leader's Toolkit** for each chapter, featuring presentation slides including our key data visualizations and talking points in the notes. These visual resources can be used as sermon illustrations, conversation starters, and even prayer reminders for pastors and church leaders at all levels.

One more way we're innovating is through a growing partnership with faculty and staff at Christian colleges and universities. This year, we are offering **Innovation Grants** to educators who care about catalyzing Bible engagement in the next generation of American adults. These small grants—ranging from $5,000 to $15,000—will be directed to Christian scholars from across the church who are willing to test innovative approaches to Bible ministry that benefit young adults on their campuses and in their broader communities. You can learn more about them at stateofthebible.org/facultygrants.

These research grants, videos, podcasts, slide decks, and other resources are an invitation for you to join us in innovative Bible ministry and find the most effective ways to care for our neighbors.

STATE OF THE BIBLE: USA 2025

Throughout 2025, the *State of the Bible* research team will be presenting a new set of findings from our January 2025 national survey. We will release new chapters from April through December 2025, each focusing on key aspects of America's relationship with the Bible, faith, and the church. Here are a few of the stories we will be releasing in the coming months:

2025 APR   **The Bible in America.** Our first chapter tracks key metrics about Bible use and Scripture engagement in the United States. We also explore the preferences for formats and digital platforms of Bible users and examine changes in the perception of the Bible.

2025 MAY   **The Bible Around the World.** We compare perspectives about the Bible in the U.S. with global ones to identify similarities and differences in Bible access and engagement across cultures. We see how Americans' views and practices regarding the Bible differ or align with people in other countries.

2025 JUN   **Human Flourishing.** In partnership with Human Flourishing researchers at Harvard University, we continue our ongoing investigation of how the Bible, faith, and the church are connected to holistic well-being.

2025

JUL

Self-Care and Well-Being. This chapter focuses on challenges to well-being and the role of the Bible in pastoral care—and self-care. Topics include loneliness, trauma and suffering, forgiveness, and the role of faith and hope. We also explore how Bible users manage stress differently than other Americans.

2025

AUG

Church Engagement. In recent years, researchers have observed significant changes in Americans' church attendance and views on the church as an institution in society. We explore both positive and negative perceptions of the church.

2025

SEP

Identity. In this chapter, we look at how engaging with the Bible shapes the identity development of Gen Z as they navigate challenges and opportunities. We'll look at how individuals from Gen Z who actively engage with the Bible search for and discover their identity.

2025

OCT

Trust. This month we assess how much trust Americans place in other people and in institutions. We explore the difference in the way Bible users place their trust compared to those who do not actively engage with the Bible.

2025

NOV

Love and Generosity. We look at how Bible engagement goes beyond shaping religious beliefs and practices and extends into everyday actions. We examine how the Bible guides people in their relationships with others and how those interactions reflect biblical values of love and generosity.

2025

DEC

Looking Back and Looking Forward. We wrap up this year's *State of the Bible* report with a review of key findings from 2025 and a preview of new topics for 2026. With a review of the highlights, we share the current landscape of Bible interest and engagement to help ministry leaders understand their audiences and more deeply engage them with God's Word.

Throughout this year's digital—and printed—book, watch for the linked **extended content**. Our new podcast will feature interviews on subject-matter experts for every chapter. We are glad to serve you with ongoing innovative *State of the Bible* material at our website, StateoftheBible.org, as well as this traditional report. There's much more to come!

CONCLUSION

As you read our 2025 report, I pray that you are encouraged by the good news that Bible use is increasing across America, particularly among demographic groups that have traditionally been the least engaged. I invite you to prayerfully consider how God may use you during this time of growing openness to the Gospel. Do you have family, friends, co-workers or neighbors who may be more willing than ever to hear the Good News found in the pages of Scripture?

Ultimately, The *State of the Bible: USA* research project is more than just a snapshot of America's spiritual state in 2025. It is an invitation and a challenge to all of us who have been impacted by the good news of the Bible to share its treasures with those around us.

JOHN FARQUHAR PLAKE, PH.D.

Dr. John Plake is a researcher with a pastor's heart. He bridges the worlds of social science, business intelligence, and spiritual formation, helping Christian leaders understand how people grow in Christ.

Dr. Plake serves as Chief Innovation Officer at American Bible Society and is the editor-in-chief of the *State of the Bible* series. Over 35 years of full-time ministry, John has served as a pastor, missionary, professor, and researcher.

He is an ordained minister with a Ph.D. in intercultural studies. He lives with his family in Wilmington, Delaware.

Contact him at
jplake@americanbible.org

CHAPTER 1

THE BIBLE IN AMERICA TODAY

*After the success of "The Chosen," Amazon and Netflix
are converting Bible stories into films and
TV shows with "Game of Thrones"-style intrigue
and romantic comedy elements.*

The New York Times[1]

The story of Jesus, presented in the multi-season serial *The Chosen*, has become a smash hit in recent years. Now there are other Bible-based dramas in the works, covering the stories of Ruth, David, and Mary the mother of Jesus, with even more on the horizon. The *Times* article notes that "other studios are eager to adapt material that has zero copyright protection and billions of adherents."[2]

---

1 https://www.nytimes.com/2025/03/02/arts/television/house-of-david-the-chosen-amazon-prime-netflix.html
2 Ibid.

For decades, religious companies have produced faith-based films that found churchgoing audiences. But *The Chosen* has pushed far beyond that. Its producing team "estimates that the show has been watched by more than 280 million unique viewers worldwide, *a third of whom it says are not religious.*"[3]

This "not religious" audience intrigues us. That's 90 million-plus, in the U.S. and elsewhere, who presumably are not Bible readers, yet have tuned in to a creative, Bible-based account of the life and teachings of Jesus.

Whatever your opinion of *The Chosen*, its popularity raises a question for anyone interested in how Americans connect with the Bible. Could *The Chosen*—or other similar presentations in the future— have a significant effect on the people we call Bible Disengaged or non-Bible Users or Non-Practicing Christians?

America's relationship with the Bible took a serious downturn a few years ago, and it has wallowed in a statistical trough ever since. This year we see a slight uptick. Is this a reversal of a previous trend? Time will tell. Significantly, we see the greatest increases among Millennials and men, populations that have previously scored low in Bible Use and Scripture Engagement. There's also been a Bible boost in formerly resistant regions—the Northeast and West. Even adherents of non-Christian religions are turning to the Bible more often.

Can we credit a particular TV show or ad campaign with these increases? Our research does not directly address motivations, but it is clear that people are looking for answers . . . increasingly in visual

3 Ibid. Italics ours.

media. These sorts of public presentations reinforce the quietly faithful lives and creative outreach of millions of Christians eager to share with their neighbors the "greatest story ever told."

BIBLE USE

We define Bible Users as those who connect with Scripture on their own at least three times a year, "not including times when you are at a large church service or Mass." This is a low bar, but it does reflect a personal decision to interact, at least occasionally, with the Bible.

From 2011 to 2021, nearly half of all Americans qualified as Bible Users, with little change from year to year. In 2022, Bible Use fell dramatically (from 50% to 40%), and it kept sliding. Our 2024 survey found only 38 percent of American adults were Bible Users, falling below even those who said they "never use the Bible" (40%).

Adult Bible Users, 2019–2025

■ Millions ●— Percentage

Year	Millions	Percentage
2019	124	49%
2020	123	48%
2021	128	50%
2022	103	40%
2023	100	39%
2024	99	38%
2025	110	41%

But this year there's better news: 10 million *more* American adults are Bible Users. The total amount of 110 million represents 41 percent of the adult population. This is the highest total since our 2021 report.[4]

Frequency of Bible Use

How often do you use the Bible?

Every day	9%
Four or more times a week	3%
Several times a week	7%
Once a week	6%
Once a month	7%
Three or four times a year	9%
Twice a year or less	21%
Never	38%

25% Weekly Bible Users

41% Bible Users

GENERATION AND GENDER

This might surprise you. **Millennials** are leading the way in this move toward greater Bible Use, and in every generation **men** are using the Bible more.

In the 2024 report, Millennials trailed all other generations, with only three in ten (30%) qualifying as Bible Users. This year they've

---

4 The *State of the Bible* survey is conducted in January, so many of its findings reflect situations from the previous year.

jumped to nearly four in ten (39%), surpassing their younger sib-
lings in Generation Z. Both male and female Millennials have seen
a substantial year-to-year increase.

Bible Users 2024–2025 by Generation[5] and Gender

■ 2024 ■ 2025

	Gen Z (adults)	Millennials	Gen X	Boomers+	Total Population
2024	36%	30%	37%	45%	38%
2025	36%	39%	42%	46%	41%

	Male Gen Z (adults)	Male Millennials	Male Gen X	Male Boomers+	Total Male
2024	33%	32%	34%	37%	34%
2025	35%	40%	44%	43%	41%

	Female Gen Z (adults)	Female Millennials	Female Gen X	Female Boomers+	Total Female
2024	41%	28%	41%	51%	41%
2025	38%	38%	41%	49%	42%

5 See the Definitions section for the current ages of each generation. Note that the Boomers+ now also
   includes the group previously known as Elders.

In all other generations, women have held steady or decreased slightly in their Bible Use, while men had substantial gains. In Gen X, men had a ten-point rise in percentage of Bible Users, while women in that generation saw no increase at all. In that age group, men forged ahead of women in Bible Use (now 44% to 41%).

Overall, in the past year, men have nearly closed the gender gap in Bible Use, turning a seven-point gulf (41% to 34% in 2024) to a slim one-point deficit (42% to 41%).

Bible Users by Generation, 2022–2025

Gen Z (adults)   Millennials   Gen X   Boomers+

REGION, RACE, RELIGION

The Southern U.S. consistently leads the way in measures of Bible Use and Scripture Engagement. In 2025 the South once again boasts the highest percentage of Bible Users (48%), with a very slight increase over 2024, but its lead is shrinking. *Every other region in the U.S. has increased its share of Bible Users by five or six points in the last year*, even the often-resistant Northeast.

Bible Users by Region, 2024–2025

West		Midwest		South		Northeast	
2024	2025	2024	2025	2024	2025	2024	2025
33%	39%	34%	39%	47%	48%	28%	33%

Two out of three Black Americans (68%) are Bible Users, by far the highest proportion of any ethnic group in our survey. Every group except Hispanics shows a substantial increase in Bible Users in the past year.

Bible Users by Race/Ethnicity,[6] 2024–2025

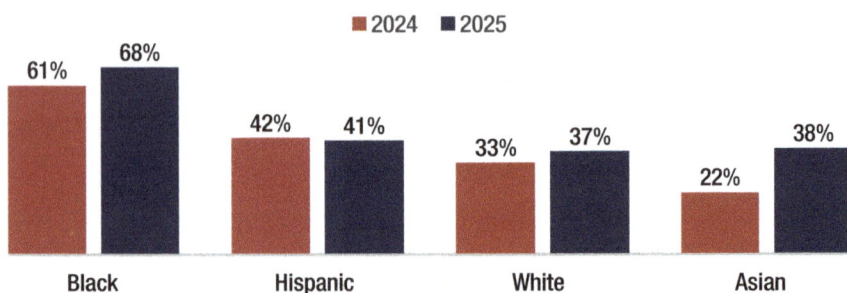

■ 2024 ■ 2025

	Black	Hispanic	White	Asian
2024	61%	42%	33%	22%
2025	68%	41%	37%	38%

Nearly three-quarters of those attending Evangelical Protestant (73%) or Historically Black Protestant churches (72%) are Bible Users. Every denominational group has an increase in Bible Users over 2024, most notably the Historically Black Protestants moving up nine points from 63 percent in 2024. The most surprising finding is that nearly half of those in "other religions" (that is, non-Christian religions) qualify as Bible Users, interacting with the Bible at least three times in the previous year.

Bible Users by Religion,[7] 2024–2025

■ 2024 ■ 2025

	Evangelical Protestant	Mainline Protestant	Historically Black Protestant	Roman Catholic	Other Religion	None
2024	72%	41%	63%	31%	30%	7%
2025	73%	41%	72%	34%	49%	5%

---

6 A number of ethnic designations are excluded in this analysis because the sample sizes are too small to provide reliable data.

7 An additional category, "Other Christian and Orthodox Christian," had too few respondents to assemble reliable data. "Other Religion" includes non-Christian religions like Judaism, Hinduism, Islam, and Buddhism.

In addition to denominational connection, we look at how deeply people interact with their churches. For several years, we have used the designation Practicing Christians for those who (1) say they're Christian, (2) attend church (in person or online) at least once a month, and (3) consider their faith "very important" to them. About a fifth of Americans are Practicing Christians.

Last year we used these same factors to identify two other groups of people. Nominal Christians call themselves Christian but don't attend church even monthly. Casual Christians attend, but they don't consider their faith "very important." And a substantial group of Non-Christians (34% of the population) does not claim to be Christian and generally doesn't participate in a church. These categories combine within a measure we call Faith Participation.

How many at each of these levels qualify as Bible Users? The percentages are starkly different. One in six (16%) Non-Christians are Bible Users, as well as nearly a third of Nominal Christians (32%). About two-thirds of Casual Christians (66%) are Bible Users, along with nearly all (92%) Practicing Christians.

Bible Users by Faith Participation Segments

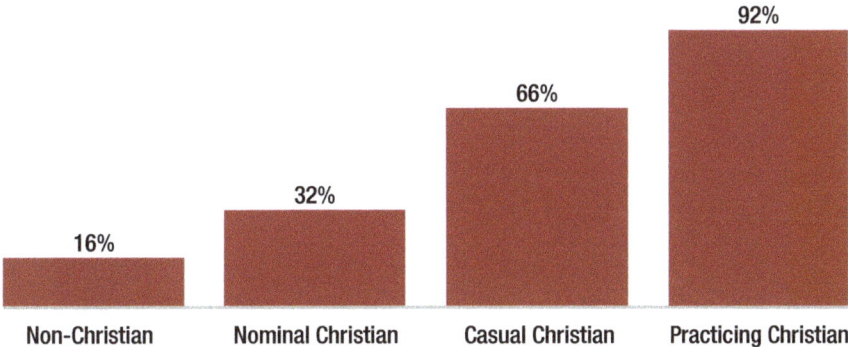

Non-Christian	Nominal Christian	Casual Christian	Practicing Christian
16%	32%	66%	92%

SCRIPTURE ENGAGEMENT

Where Bible Use represents a rather low commitment, as little as three readings a year, Scripture Engagement is a far more robust category. It merges frequency of Bible reading with other measures of the Bible's role in people's lives. We look at the *centrality* of the Bible in people's decision-making and its *impact* on people's relationships with God and others. Responses to fourteen questions on these matters create a score, which then qualifies a respondent as Scripture Engaged, Movable Middle, or Bible Disengaged.

Scripture Engagement, 2019–2025

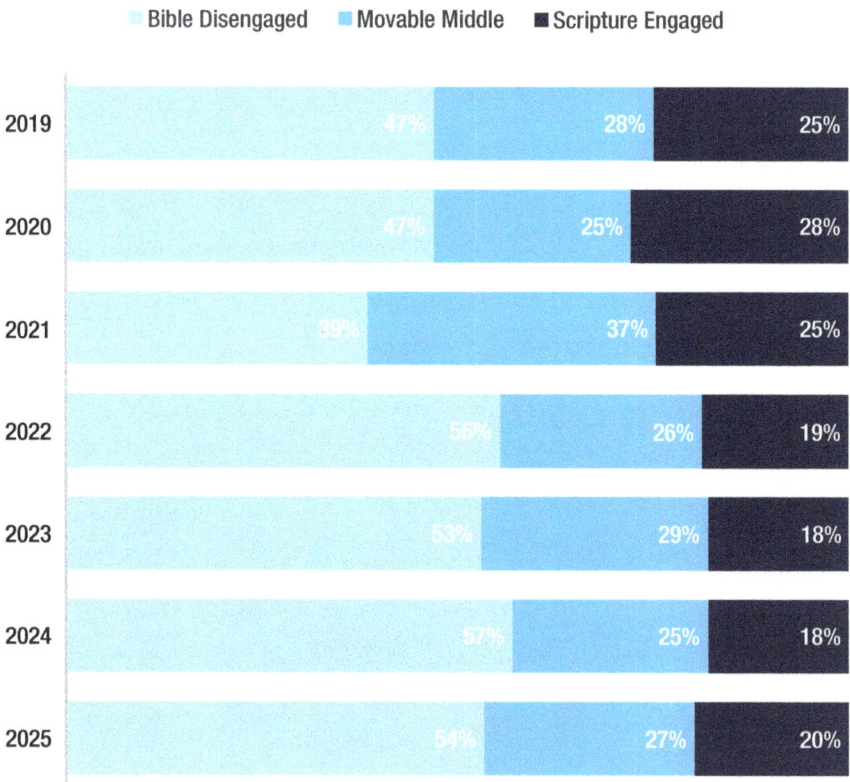

Bible Disengaged ■ Movable Middle ■ Scripture Engaged

Year	Bible Disengaged	Movable Middle	Scripture Engaged
2019	47%	28%	25%
2020	47%	25%	28%
2021	39%	37%	25%
2022	56%	26%	19%
2023	53%	29%	18%
2024	57%	25%	18%
2025	54%	27%	20%

In recent years, Scripture Engagement has been in the same statistical trough as Bible Use. The survey taken in January 2022 showed a major spike in the number of Bible Disengaged, and both the Movable Middle and Scripture Engaged suffered big losses. The next two surveys showed no improvement.

This year, however, there's a glimmer of good news. The percentage of Scripture Engaged has edged upward (to 20%)—still not back to 2021 levels, but moving in the right direction. Last year, 47 million Americans qualified as Scripture Engaged; this year there are more than 52 million.

SCRIPTURE ENGAGEMENT AND THE CHURCH

The Bible repeatedly touts the value of the community of faith, urging us not to "give up the habit of meeting together" (Hebrews 10:25). While it's possible for someone to be Scripture Engaged and not go to church, it's rather rare. Only one in eight of the Scripture Engaged (12%) are unchurched.

Earlier in this chapter, we reviewed Faith Participation segments, including the categories of Nominal Christians (the 57% of self-identified Christians who seldom attend church) and Casual Christians (the 16% of Christians who attend but don't consider their faith "very important"). The connection between Scripture Engagement and church involvement becomes even clearer when we examine these categories.

More than two of three (68%) Practicing Christians are also Scripture Engaged, with about a quarter (26%) in the Movable Middle and very few (6%) Disengaged. Nominal Christians show the reverse, with the great majority Bible Disengaged. What's most fascinating is how the Movable Middle (53%) owns the Casual Christian category, and that makes sense. These people are in church, but their faith is not very important to them. In the same way, they may read the Bible occasionally, but they seem to hold its teachings at arm's length, not fully committing.

Faith Participation Segment by Scripture Engagement

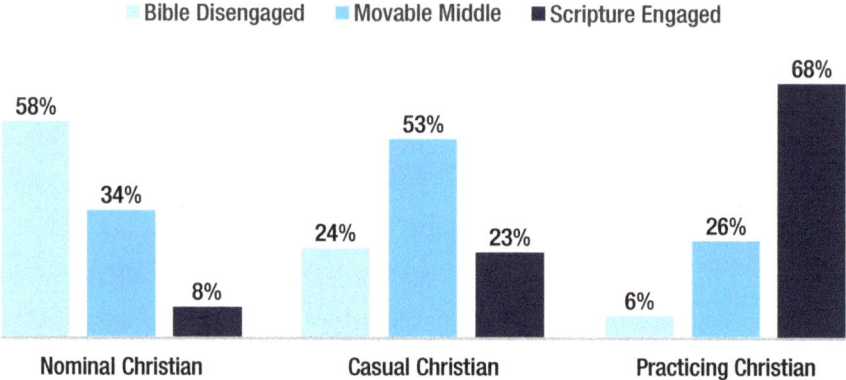

Legend: Bible Disengaged ■ Movable Middle ■ Scripture Engaged

	Nominal Christian	Casual Christian	Practicing Christian
Bible Disengaged	58%	24%	6%
Movable Middle	34%	53%	26%
Scripture Engaged	8%	23%	68%

EXAMINING KEY DEMOGRAPHICS

Where does the 2025 rise in Scripture Engagement come from? The two youngest generations. While they are still the least-engaged age groups, both have increased by about a third over last year (11% to 15% for Gen Z and 12% to 17% for Millennials).

While Generation X shows a minor decrease in Scripture Engagement (21% to 20%), there seems to be a major relocation in that group from the Disengaged to the Movable Middle.

Black Americans were already leading the way in Scripture Engagement by a large margin, yet they had a major rise in that category (from 27% to 36%). Their percentage of Scripture Engaged is now twice that of any other major ethnic group (36% to 18% for Whites and Hispanics). Asian-Americans had a major shift from the Bible Disengaged up to the Movable Middle, and a substantial rise in the Scripture Engaged. White Americans also had gains in the Scripture Engaged and Movable Middle, with a corresponding drop in the Bible Disengaged.

ACCESS, APPROACHES, AND ATTITUDES

How do people interact with Scripture, and why? The *State of the Bible* survey includes questions about technology, reading habits, and beliefs about the Bible.

More than three in four Americans say they own a Bible (77%, up from 74% last year), and virtually all of these people say it's "in a language and format they understand." For most of its history, American Bible Society has focused on making sure people had Bibles, but the digital revolution has changed that playing field.[8] Now, if you have a smartphone or computer, you essentially own a Bible.

But are people using that technology? Increasingly, yes. Two thirds of Bible Users (66%) say they access the Bible digitally at least some of the time, with higher numbers among younger generations.

---

8 American Bible Society is now at the heart of digital Bible use around the world through its stewardship of the Digital Bible Library.

These days people have three broad choices when accessing information or entertainment . . . or the Bible. We can read it as text, we can listen to audio content, or we can watch video. Our survey asked how often people access the Bible in these three general formats.

We're especially interested in the Movable Middle, because this is where future growth in Scripture Engagement will come from. We're also curious about the media preferences of different generations.

You won't be surprised that Gen Z, our youngest group, shows the greatest preference for video content, with nearly three of five (59%) in the Movable Middle accessing such content at least monthly. Guess which generation leads in the monthly reading of Bible text. Millennials, at 70 percent.

As we seek to draw more of the Movable Middle into Scripture Engagement, especially in these low-engaging age groups, Bible communicators might consider two courses of action. First, provide more Bible content on video to meet the clear preferences of Gen Z. Second, let Millennials know that quality Bible content also exists in video and audio formats.

When people of all these generations access Bible content online, what platforms do they use? (We're not just including those in the Movable Middle now, but all those who say they use the Bible online at least some of the time.) Three out of five digital Bible Users (62%) say they click on "Bible apps" (such as YouVersion). The next most popular options, a "Bible-based website" and YouTube, get about half that traffic (30% and 27% respectively).

Generations have distinctive platform preferences. While every age group seems to like Bible apps, those in our oldest generation, Boomers+, specialize in what we might consider classic technology—not only TV and radio, but websites and Facebook. Those in Gen X often find their Bible content on YouTube; Millennials on Instagram. While it's no surprise that TikTok reaches our youngest generation far more than our oldest (24% to 1%), Gen Z also enjoys Bible content on podcasts—in fact it's their second most favored option (at 33%, with 59% using Bible apps).

It's worth remembering that our survey only includes adults over 18 years of age, so a third of Gen Z is not included here . . . yet. In the coming years we expect their preferred media to rise in these rankings.

Bible Access by Media Format and Generation

"How often do you interact with Bible content in the following formats?"

Text   Audio   Video

	Text	Audio	Video
Gen Z (adults)	49%	47%	59%
Millennials	70%	46%	46%
Gen X	60%	27%	36%
Boomers+	63%	35%	39%

Base = Movable Middle digital Bible Users reporting using one of these formats at least monthly

Digital Bible Platform Preferences

On which of the following platforms do you most often interact with Bible content?

	Overall Percentage	Leading generation	Lowest generation
Bible app	62%	Millennials (67%)	Gen Z (59%)
Bible-based website	30%	Boomers (40%)	Millennials (25%)
YouTube	27%	Gen X (31%)	Boomers+ (20%)
Podcast/Webcast	21%	Gen Z (33%)	Boomers+ (14%)
Facebook	16%	Gen X (19%)	Gen Z (8%)
TV/Radio	14%	Boomers+ (22%)	Gen Z (8%)
Instagram	8%	Millennials (15%)	Boomers+ (3%)
TikTok	8%	Gen Z (24%)	Boomers+ (1%)

Note: Respondents could choose multiple options
Base: Bible Users who use digital platforms

METHODS OF BIBLE READING

For a few years now, we have asked people about their Bible reading practices—not just frequency but details of how they conduct their time with Scripture.

- I do it at about the same time of the day.
- I participate in a Bible study group.
- I read one or more chapters or a complete story.
- I follow a reading guide, schedule, plan, or program.
- *I read a few verses at a time.*
- *I select Bible passages based on my mood at the time.*

Those who are less Scripture engaged choose the last two statements more than the first four. We characterize the first four as "disciplined" Bible reading—requiring commitment to a group, a schedule, a plan, or a longer text. We call the last two options "casual" Bible reading. While the Bible benefits committed and casual readers alike, those who are most transformed by Scripture tend to go beyond grabbing a few mood-appropriate verses.

The 2025 survey has confirmed this pattern, with Scripture Engaged people generally doubling up on the Movable Middle on those first four statements.

For years we've noticed a recurring anomaly. When we ask whether people's Bible reading increased or decreased in the previous year, more people say they've increased (usually 15% claiming increase with 10% admitting decrease). This has occurred consistently, even in years when Bible reading was dropping. But this year it's not just wishful thinking: Bible Use has actually increased.

Speaking of wishful thinking, we also ask respondents, "Do you wish you read the Bible more?" Just over half of all Americans (51%) say yes (a couple of ticks down from last year's 53%). As you might expect, the Scripture Engaged can't get enough of God's Word. Seven of eight (88%) say they wish they read it more. Only a quarter of the Bible Disengaged (26%) have this wish; it's just not that important to most of them. But that Movable Middle group (80%) comes close to the Engaged in their desire for more Bible reading. To be sure, there can be many obstacles between wish and reality, but this is a positive factor. It's what makes this group movable.

ABOUT THE BIBLE

Besides all the data on formats and practices in Bible use, we also want to know what people believe *about* the Bible. We present five statements in random order and ask participants which comes closest to their view. For those who say the Bible is "just another book of teachings," we ask if they agree with another, more negative, statement: *The Bible was written to control or manipulate other people.*

Taken together, these responses give us a sense of the terrain of American attitudes toward the Bible, from traditional to modernist and even antagonistic.

Attitudes about the Bible, 2025

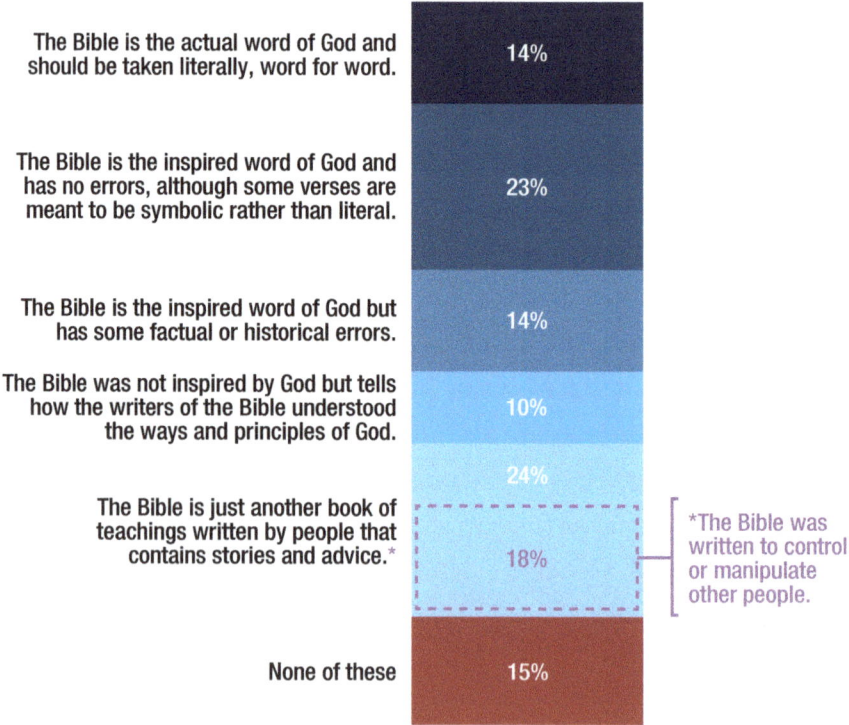

Statement	%
The Bible is the actual word of God and should be taken literally, word for word.	14%
The Bible is the inspired word of God and has no errors, although some verses are meant to be symbolic rather than literal.	23%
The Bible is the inspired word of God but has some factual or historical errors.	14%
The Bible was not inspired by God but tells how the writers of the Bible understood the ways and principles of God.	10%
	24%
The Bible is just another book of teachings written by people that contains stories and advice.*	18%
None of these	15%

*The Bible was written to control or manipulate other people.

CONCLUSION

More than half of Americans (56%) say they are curious about the Bible and/or Jesus. Even among the youngest generations, Gen Z and Millennials, half of them say they're curious. Among the Movable Middle, that neutral group brimming with possibility, more than four out of five (82%) confess curiosity about the Bible or Jesus or both.

What can we do about that?

You might be afraid that people don't want to hear the good news. You might assume that everyone in your community is part of that 18 percent who are sure that the Bible was written to control and manipulate. It's a shame that those people think that, and maybe someday we can convince them otherwise, but three times as many people are longing to know more. How will we satisfy that desire? We see in this year's data a move toward Scripture, especially in previously resistant groups. For Christian leaders, communicators, artists, and servants, this is a time to talk about the deep wonder we find in the Bible, to live out its teachings with compassion and wholeness, and to welcome others into its rich wisdom. ◼

ARE MORE PEOPLE USING THE BIBLE?

Our first interview of 2025 is with **Jennifer Holloran**, President and CEO of American Bible Society, talking about why Bible use might be on the rise. Click on or follow the QR code to listen now, and subscribe to this new podcast series to hear future conversations about the State of the Bible in America.

Bible Use

29% ↑
increase in Bible use among Millennials

19% ↑
increase in Bible use among Men

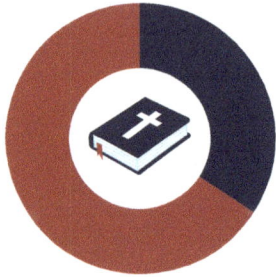

TOP 3
Platforms of Digital Bible Users

62% Bible App

30% Bible Website

27% YouTube

66%
of Bible users access the Bible digitally

34%
of Bible users access the Bible only in print

10 MILLION
more people are Bible users in 2025 compared to last year

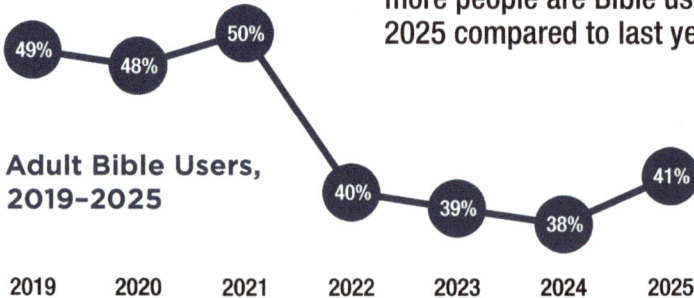

Adult Bible Users, 2019–2025

49% — 48% — 50% — 40% — 39% — 38% — 41%

2019   2020   2021   2022   2023   2024   2025

DEFINITION

Bible Users are individuals who interact with the Bible on their own at least three times a year.

CHAPTER 2

THE BIBLE AROUND THE WORLD

> *"We must be global Christians with a global vision*
> *because our God is a global God."*
>
> *John Stott* [1]

A t various moments in history, Christians have pushed harder toward a global vision. You might look to the Moravian outreach beginning in the 1720s or William Carey's challenge to the British church in the 1790s or the 1806 Haystack Prayer Meeting that launched an American missionary movement.

Half a century ago, the Lausanne Conference of 1974 brought together 2,700 Christian leaders from 150 different nations to discuss world evangelization. Billy Graham used his worldwide fame to convene the crowd, and British pastor and theologian John Stott also emerged as a leader. Yet the groundbreaking feature of the event was

---

1   Stott (1921–2011), an Anglican priest, reportedly said this often. Cited in Christopher J. H. Wright, "John Stott's Global God," *Christianity Today*, January/February 2022.

the active involvement of hundreds of international church leaders. The Lausanne Conference didn't just inspire Western Christians to carry the gospel to unreached peoples; it affirmed the work that local churches and evangelists were already doing all over the world. It was a vision-changer then, and the movement continues to shape a global vision for the church today.

This *State of the Bible* report usually focuses on statistics from the U.S. After all, we work for the American Bible Society, with a mission to promote Scripture engagement in our own country. But we also belong to the United Bible Societies (UBS), a fellowship that is active in more than 240 nations of the world. This past year, we had the opportunity to participate with our colleagues from the British and Foreign Bible Society in a global project called the Patmos Initiative. In partnership with UBS, and with the expertise of the Gallup organization, the *Patmos World Bible Attitudes Survey* polled 91,000 people in 85 countries on Bible attitudes and practices. In this chapter, we compare Bible use, attitudes, and interest in the U.S. to the rest of the world, with a focus on other countries in "the Secular West," to gain a better picture of how God is working around the world, as well as continuing needs and opportunities for Bible access and engagement.[2]

CLUSTERS

In the last book of the Bible, John writes from exile on the isle of Patmos (Revelation 1:9) to seven churches of Asia Minor, each with a distinct profile and unique challenges (Revelation 2—3). Drawing

---

2 Data in this chapter are taken by permission from *The Patmos World Bible Attitudes Survey* (2025). Gallup is the source research agency for *The Patmos World Bible Attitudes Survey.* Fieldwork details for all countries can be read in the methodology chapter of *The Patmos Survey* report: patmos.bfbs.org.

inspiration from this, the Patmos Initiative identifies seven "clusters" of countries. Each cluster shares a distinct profile and unique challenges with regard to the Bible and Christian faith.

Seven Clusters of the Patmos Initiative

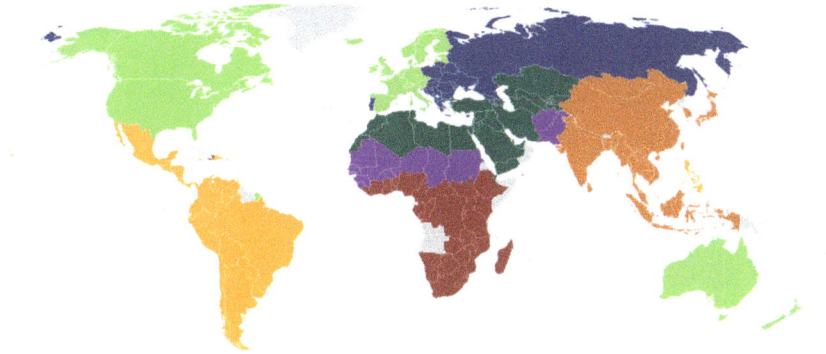

	Geography	Religion
Cluster 1	West Africa, Chad, Sudan, Pakistan, Afghanistan	Majority Muslim
Cluster 2	Russia, Eastern Europe, Portugal	Majority Christian
Cluster 3	North Africa, Middle East, Turkey, Central Asia	Majority Muslim
Cluster 4	Latin America, Caribbean, Philippines	Majority Christian
Cluster 5	USA, Canada, Western Europe, Australia, New Zealand	"The Secular West"
Cluster 6	India, China, Indonesia, Japan	Religiously diverse
Cluster 7	Sub-Saharan Africa	Majority Christian

Map Credit: The Patmos Initiative

Clusters 1 and 3 spread across the Sahel, North Africa, and the Middle East, up into Central Asia. The Muslim faith dominates these areas, with strong commitment to that religion and, generally, resistance to Christianity. Countries in Cluster 1 face significant poverty. Cluster 3 is marked by political authoritarianism. The Patmos pollsters couldn't even ask about the Bible in many of these countries, yet they found openness to explore new ideas among two groups: secular Muslims (especially in central Asia) and Muslims practicing their own faith but curious about other religions.

Cluster 2 (Russia, Eastern Europe, and Portugal) has a strong historical connection to Orthodox Christianity, but this doesn't always mean active personal commitment.

Cluster 5, including the U.S., Western Europe, Canada, Australia, and New Zealand, earns the moniker "the Secular West." Growing secularization has eroded the region's historical commitment to Christianity. Young people are less likely to identify as Christian, but when they do, they tend to practice it faithfully—more than most older adults who identify with Christianity more but practice it less. (Later in this chapter, we'll compare the U.S. with other countries in Cluster 5.)

Cluster 6, in eastern Asia, groups together the most populous nations on earth. Several of the world's large religions are prevalent here—including Buddhism, Hinduism, and Islam. Only 6 percent say they are interested in learning about the Christian Bible. This might be because three quarters of those in this cluster (76%) say they know nothing about the Bible and more than half (56%) have never even heard of it.

Cluster 4 (mostly Latin America) with its strong Roman Catholic heritage, shows high appreciation for and interaction with the Bible, though we see growing secularism among the younger generations. Cluster 7, most of sub-Saharan Africa, shows high interest in the Bible. Nine of ten are interested in learning more about it, and Bible use is high.

AUDIENCE GROUPS IN ALL CLUSTERS

Besides identifying clusters of countries with similar profiles, the Patmos Initiative also evaluates the populations of those clusters in terms of their openness to the Bible or to new religious ideas (other than the dominant religion). Based on survey responses, seven "audience groups" emerge.

- Actively engaged and committed to the Bible
- Open to learning more about the Bible
- Indifferent to the Bible
- Closed to the Bible
- Receptive to new ideas or other religions
- Indifferent to new ideas or other religions
- Closed to new ideas or other religions

Each cluster has a unique configuration of these seven audience groups. Appreciating the contexts in which they work can allow church leaders and Bible organizations to tailor their ministry more effectively. For instance, in areas where nearly everyone follows a religion other than Christianity, many know nothing about the Bible. This makes "openness to the Bible" a moot point. But even in those cultures there might be openness to new religious ideas, such as Christianity.

Audience Groups by Cluster

- ■ Actively engaged and committed to the Bible
- ■ Open to learning more about the Bible
- ■ Indifferent to the Bible
- ■ Closed to or dismissive of the Bible

- ■ Receptive to new ideas and other religions
- ■ Indifferent to new ideas and other religions
- ■ Closed to new ideas and other religions

Cluster 1 (Majority Muslim): West Africa, Chad, Sudan, Pakistan, Afghanistan

Cluster 2 (Majority Christian): Russia, Eastern Europe, Portugal

Cluster 3 (Majority Muslim): North Africa, Middle East, Turkey, Central Asia

Cluster 4 (Majority Christian): Latin America, Caribbean, Philippines

Cluster 5 ("The Secular West"): US, Western Europe, Australia, New Zealand

Cluster 6 (Religiously diverse): India, China, Indonesia, Japan

Cluster 7 (Majority Christian): Sub-Saharan Africa

BIBLE AND CHURCH IN THE SECULAR WEST

We now focus on Cluster 5, the Secular West, which includes the U.S. and Western Europe, as well as other English-speaking nations (Canada, Australia, New Zealand). How do all these countries stack up in their Bible Use and church attendance? What Bible formats do they prefer? Later we'll also examine a range of attitudes about the Bible.

Bible Use by Country (selected countries in Cluster 5)[3]

"How often do you use the Bible?"

■ Never   ■ Occasionally   ■ At least monthly   ■ A few times a week or more

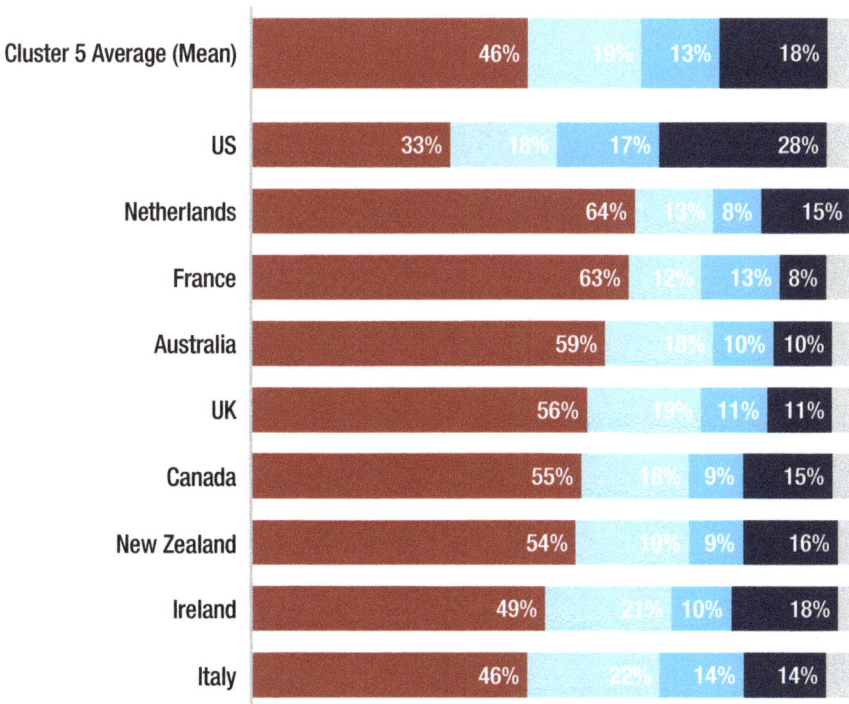

Country	Never	Occasionally	At least monthly	A few times a week or more
Cluster 5 Average (Mean)	46%	19%	13%	18%
US	33%	18%	17%	28%
Netherlands	64%	13%	8%	15%
France	63%	12%	13%	8%
Australia	59%	18%	10%	10%
UK	56%	19%	11%	11%
Canada	55%	18%	9%	15%
New Zealand	54%	19%	9%	16%
Ireland	49%	21%	10%	18%
Italy	46%	22%	14%	14%

3 Does not include the 1–4% who replied, "Prefer not to say."

Bible Use is far more prevalent in the U.S. than in any other nation in the Secular West. More than half of those in every other Cluster 5 country say they never use the Bible (except for Italy and Ireland, with 46% and 49%). But only one in three Americans say they never use the Bible (33%), with more than a quarter (28%) interacting with it at least a few times a week.

France (only 8% turning to the Bible weekly) and the Netherlands (64% with no Bible use) are among the least Bible-connected countries. Sweden (63% "never") and Norway (only 5% a few times a week or more) also score low on this question.

Church Attendance by Country
(selected countries in Cluster 5)

"Apart from weddings, baptisms/christenings and funerals, how often did you go to a Christian church service either online or in person, in the past 12 months?"

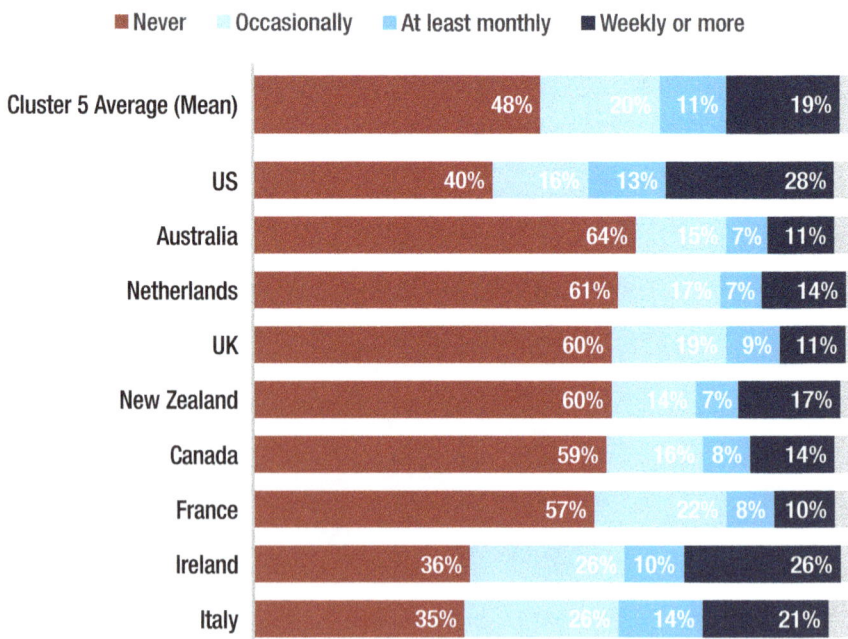

■ Never ■ Occasionally ■ At least monthly ■ Weekly or more

Country	Never	Occasionally	At least monthly	Weekly or more
Cluster 5 Average (Mean)	48%	20%	11%	19%
US	40%	16%	13%	28%
Australia	64%	15%	7%	11%
Netherlands	61%	17%	7%	14%
UK	60%	19%	9%	11%
New Zealand	60%	14%	7%	17%
Canada	59%	18%	8%	14%
France	57%	22%	8%	10%
Ireland	36%	26%	10%	26%
Italy	35%	26%	14%	21%

It's no surprise that Bible Use tracks closely with church attendance. People who make a point of gathering with people of faith in the worship of God also tend to connect with God in Scripture on a regular basis. Our statistics confirm that.

Once again, church attendance in the U.S. (28% weekly, a total of 41% attending at least monthly) far exceeds the average for the Secular West nations (19% weekly, 30% total monthly). But notice that Italy and Ireland, two nations with a strong Roman Catholic heritage, have strong numbers in church attendance, far greater than their Bible Use. In fact, those two countries have the lowest percentage of people saying they "never" attend church.

BIBLE FORMATS

Some might expect that the general cultural shift to digital media and audiovisual content would be seen first in the developed nations of the Secular West, but throughout this cluster, people who use the Bible at least once or twice a year still prefer to read the Bible on paper or screens (68%) rather than listening to it (17%) or watching videos (12%). The Netherlands (75%) and New Zealand (74%) are most likely to prefer text, with Sweden (55%) least likely. Belgium has the highest percentage in this cluster who prefer to interact with the Bible in an audio format (28%). The lowest percentage belongs to Italy, where only one in ten (10%) prefer audio. When it comes to video, those in the United Kingdom are most likely to prefer that format (22%), with Belgium and Ireland the least likely (9%).

Preferences do not always match up with actions. The Patmos Survey also asked about the frequency of use among specific formats. How often do people consult Bible material on a phone, tablet, or computer? How many Bible readers make this a regular habit? How many watch video content about the Bible at least a few times a week?

Once again, the U.S. is slightly ahead of the average for Cluster 5 in both these media formats, but there are a number of countries ahead and behind. Ireland leads the way with digital Bible reading plans (40%), just ahead of Sweden and Belgium (37%). Italy (15%) lags behind.

Preferred Bible Formats

"How do you most prefer to access the Bible?"

	Cluster 5 Average (Mean)	US	Highest	Second	Lowest
Text	68%	70%	Netherlands, 75%	New Zealand, 74%	Sweden, 55%
Audio	17%	18%	Belgium, 28%	Sweden, 25%	Italy, 10%
Video	12%	11%	UK, 22%	Norway, 20%	Belgium, Ireland, 9%

Base: Those who use the Bible at least once or twice a year

With regard to video watching, Belgium (39%) leads the way in regular viewing of Bible content. And even though Norwegians expressed the second highest level of *preference* for video content (see above), their regular *use* of such content was the lowest in the cluster (13%).

Actual Digital Bible Use by Format

"How often have you read from a Bible reading plan on a phone, tablet, or computer?"

*"How often have you watched a Bible-oriented program
on a television, phone, tablet, or computer?"*

Responding "a few times a week" or more

	Cluster 5 Average (Mean)	US	Highest	Second	Lowest
Read from a plan	28%	30%	Ireland, 41%	Sweden, Belgium, 37%	Italy, 14%
Watched a program	26%	28%	Belgium, 39%	Ireland, 36%	Norway, 13%

Base: Those who use the Bible at least once or twice a year

ATTITUDES

One of the reasons we can define our cluster as the *Secular* West is a steady erosion of appreciation for the Bible and Christian tradition over the last century. Historically, this is the territory of Francis of Assisi, of Luther, Calvin, and Wesley. Christianity grew and thrived on these acres, but lately there's a different story being played out.

Has the church lost the hearts and minds of the people? Or is there still some appreciation for the old Scriptures, perhaps some curiosity? To find out, the Patmos Survey included various questions about people's attitudes toward the Bible and faith, both positive and negative.

What are the two major reasons why you use the Bible? This was asked of those who indicated some level of Bible use. Respondents could choose two answers from thirteen listed, or they could say "other" or opt out entirely. The top three answers from the U.S. matched those from all of Cluster 5:

- *To deepen my relationship with God* (U.S. 24%; Cluster 21%)
- *To guide me with everyday issues* (U.S. 15%; Cluster 12%)
- *To develop my spiritual life* (U.S. 14%; Cluster 13%)

American respondents were the most likely to choose the first two answers, with Norwegians being the least likely (9% and 6%). Canadians were the most likely to choose the "spiritual life" response (17%), with Switzerland least likely (4%).

Another option was: *To understand ancient cultures.* The U.S. and Canada were the least likely to choose this (4%), under the Cluster average (6%). Slovenians (15%) and Norwegians (12%) were the most likely to select this reason to read the Bible.

Is religion an important part of your daily life? Across Cluster 5, four out of ten (40%) said yes. Americans seem to be most religious (53% saying yes, with Italians close behind at 50%). The least religious country appears to be Norway (17%).

Those who answered no on the religion question received a follow-up: *Why not?* Across the board, nearly a third (31%) said they didn't believe in "any divine beings/higher powers." A fifth (20%) of the non-religionists in Cluster 5 chose as their reason "I do not think religion can be relevant to my life." Among the less popular answers was: *I have had a bad experience with religion* (6% overall, but 9% in the U.S.).

Agree or Disagree: The Bible is a source of harm in the world. Less than a quarter of the Secular West cluster (22%) agrees or strongly agrees with this, almost matching the U.S. results. But Americans seem more eager to resist this notion, far exceeding the cluster average "strongly disagreeing" (37% U.S. to 28% in the cluster). Nearly two of three Italians disagree or strongly disagree on the Bible doing harm (65%). Notably, Ireland—a very religious nation that has experienced some religion-based troubles—showed more agreement (ten points over the mean) and less disagreement (six points under the mean) regarding the harm the Bible could cause.

The Bible as a "Source of Harm," Selected Countries

"The Bible is a source of harm in the world."

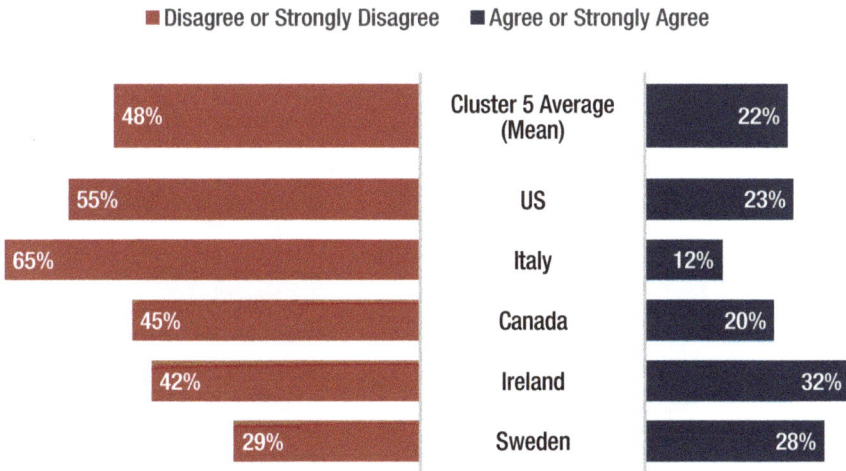

■ Disagree or Strongly Disagree   ■ Agree or Strongly Agree

48%	Cluster 5 Average (Mean)	22%
55%	US	23%
65%	Italy	12%
45%	Canada	20%
42%	Ireland	32%
29%	Sweden	28%

Agree or Disagree: It's difficult to trust the Bible because it clashes with the scientific worldview. Consider this statement for yourself. It has several components, doesn't it? In order to agree, you need to acknowledge that there is a "scientific worldview" inconsistent with the Bible's teaching. This makes it "difficult" to trust the Bible. If you disagree, are you saying the Bible is consistent with science or that there's no difficulty because each has its own domain? Or do you trust the Bible as a corrective to an overly scientific outlook? This question is especially important in the context of Western Europe with its rich history in scientific discovery and centuries of interaction between faith and science.

The U.S. is the only nation in this group with more disagreement (41%) than agreement (31%)—more who say it's *not* difficult to trust the Bible. The level of "strong" disagreement in the U.S. (23%) more than doubles that of nearly every other nation in the cluster.

The Bible and Science, Selected Countries

"It's difficult to trust the Bible because it clashes with the scientific worldview."

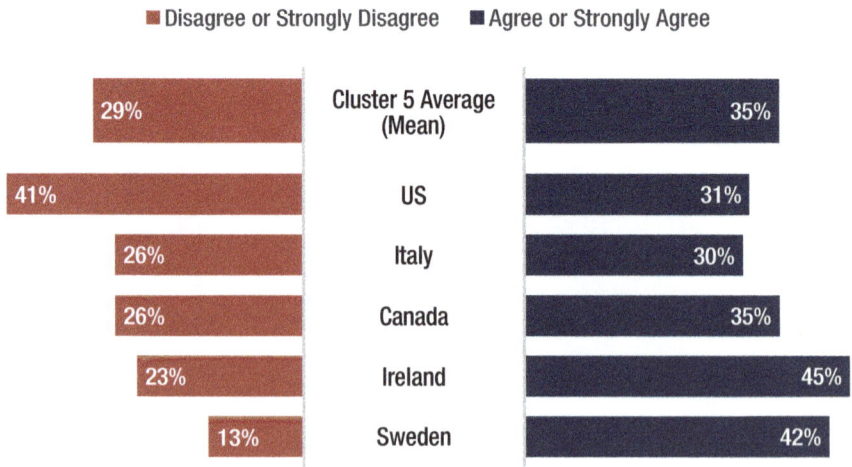

■ Disagree or Strongly Disagree   ■ Agree or Strongly Agree

Country	Disagree or Strongly Disagree	Agree or Strongly Agree
Cluster 5 Average (Mean)	29%	35%
US	41%	31%
Italy	26%	30%
Canada	26%	35%
Ireland	23%	45%
Sweden	13%	42%

Agree or Disagree: The Bible is relevant to me personally. Seldom do we find such a basic question with such devastating results. This is the crux of Bible ministry, is it not? We offer the Bible, not merely as a historical artifact, but as the wisdom of our Maker, deeply connected to the situations of our lives.

At first glance, the numbers don't look too bad. Across the cluster, a nearly equal number agree and disagree (36% and 37% mean), but those numbers are heavily influenced by strong figures from the U.S., where more than half (51%) affirm the relevance of Scripture and less than a quarter (24%) disagree. The median average for the cluster tilts strongly toward disagreement.

Clearly, Americans are outliers on this question. Italy is the only other country with more agreement (37%) than disagreement (31%). Every other country is more likely to disagree on the Bible's relevance, most by a wide margin. Sweden (59%) and Norway (58%) have the highest levels of disagreement, but we find similar numbers from the Netherlands, Germany, Switzerland, Austria, and Belgium. In all those countries, at least half of the people say the Bible is irrelevant to their lives, and less than a quarter say it's relevant.

The Bible's Relevance, Selected Countries

"The Bible is relevant to me personally."

■ Disagree or Strongly Disagree ■ Agree or Strongly Agree

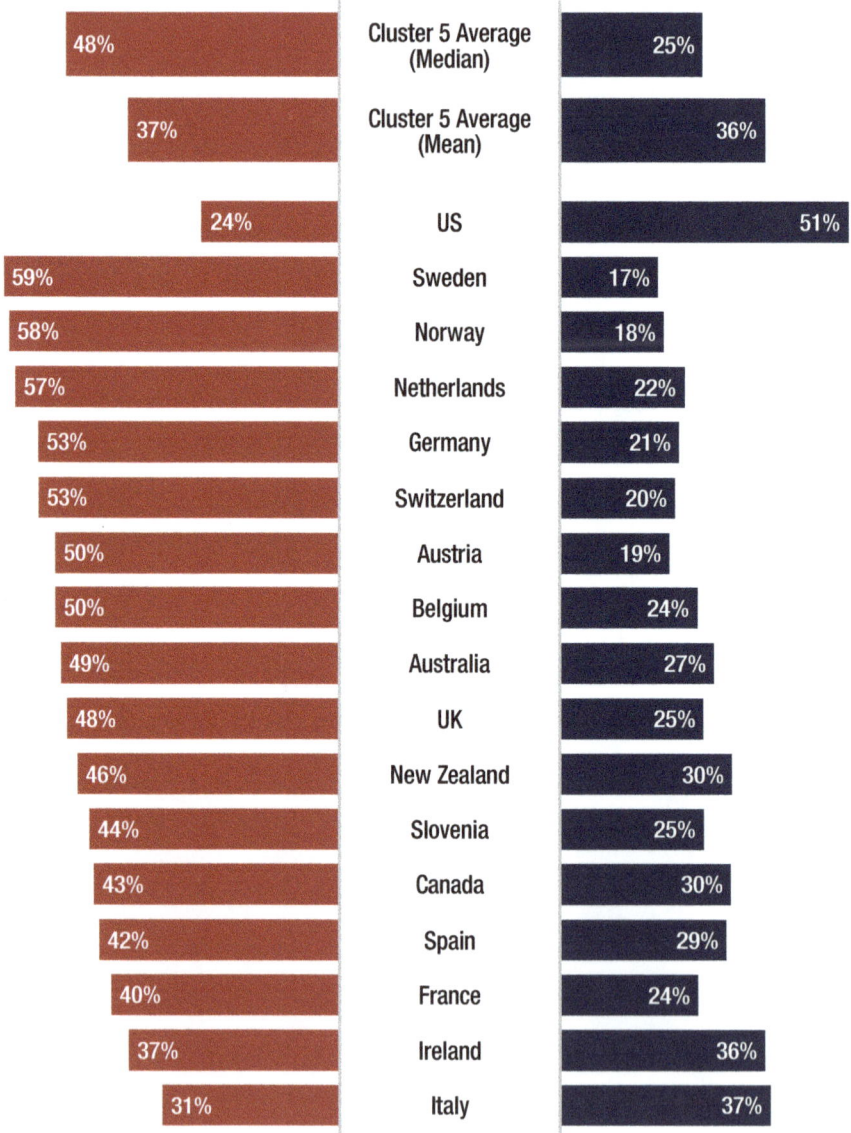

Country	Disagree or Strongly Disagree	Agree or Strongly Agree
Cluster 5 Average (Median)	48%	25%
Cluster 5 Average (Mean)	37%	36%
US	24%	51%
Sweden	59%	17%
Norway	58%	18%
Netherlands	57%	22%
Germany	53%	21%
Switzerland	53%	20%
Austria	50%	19%
Belgium	50%	24%
Australia	49%	27%
UK	48%	25%
New Zealand	46%	30%
Slovenia	44%	25%
Canada	43%	30%
Spain	42%	29%
France	40%	24%
Ireland	37%	36%
Italy	31%	37%

LEARNING AND LEADERSHIP

Are people in the Secular West interested in learning more about the Bible? If so, how do they prefer to learn, and how can church leaders help?

Overall, the survey respondents form four rather equal quadrants: very interested in learning more, somewhat interested, not very interested, and not at all interested. Each group includes between 22 and 27 percent of the population. The highest levels of interest appear in the U.S., the lowest in Sweden and Norway. (Italians also show more interest in the Bible.)

Interest in Learning About the Bible

"How interested, if at all, are you in learning more about the Bible?"

	Cluster 5 Average (Mean)	Highest	Second	Lowest
Not at all interested	27%	Sweden, 43%	Australia, 41%	Italy, 16%
Somewhat OR Very interested	45%	US, 59%	Italy, 49%	Sweden, 24%
Very interested	22%	US, 34%	Ireland, 19%	Sweden, Norway, 8%

The Patmos Survey followed up with questions about why people were or weren't interested in learning more. The top reasons for a lack of interest were: "I'm not religious" (23%) and "It's not relevant to me" (22%).

Why did others want to learn more? The top reason was "To help me grow spiritually" (19%). This was followed by "To help me know God better" (16%) and "To help me answer life's big questions" (15%). The fourth most-chosen response was especially interesting in this region of changing cultures: "To help me understand what Christians believe" (13%). This was the top answer selected in France (22%).

All who said they were "very" or "somewhat" interested in learning more about the Bible got two more questions, zeroing in on methods of learning that are desirable and effective.

Methods of Learning About the Bible

"How would you most prefer to learn about the Bible?" (top responses)

	Cluster 5 Average (Mean)	US	Highest	Second	Lowest
Online materials I can read on my own	27%	27%	Ireland, 41%	Australia, Canada, Belgium, UK, 30%	France, Germany, 21%
Attending a Christian church service	17%	21%	US, 21%	Switzerland, 19%	Belgium, 6%
Meeting in person with a group of people	15%	13%	Italy, 21%	France, 20%	Switzerland, 10%
Watching videos about the Bible, either online or in some other way	11%	10%	Italy, 17%	Sweden, Norway, Slovenia, 13%	Ireland, 6%

Respondents showed a strong preference (27%) for "Online materials I can read on my own," especially in Ireland (41%). That was the most-selected method in every country. Americans were the most likely people to choose "Attending a Christian church service" as a method of learning about the Bible.

The survey also asked this group, "What would most help you learn more about the Bible?" Eleven options were offered, and we saw fairly even distribution among the responses. The top six were:

- Something that helps relate the Bible to everyday life (14%)
- Talking with Christians (13%)
- Short reflections about the Bible (11%)
- Talking to Bible experts (10%)
- Something that breaks the Bible down into manageable pieces (10%)
- Talking with like-minded people (10%)

Of course there are many helpful ways a person can learn about the Bible. Leadership is an important part of that process. Are church leaders throughout the Secular West helping people connect with the Bible? Are leaders helping people "relate the Bible to everyday life"? The Patmos Survey asked those questions and found the majority of church attenders throughout this cluster feel that their church leaders are both making the Bible relevant and encouraging people to read it for themselves.

That same group of church attenders was asked whether they agreed that "Church leaders often make the Bible relevant to my life." In most countries, the percentages of those agreeing run a few ticks higher. The average (mean) level of agreement is 67 percent.

Church Leaders Encouraging Bible Reading

"Church leaders encourage me to read the Bible"

Percent agreeing or strongly agreeing

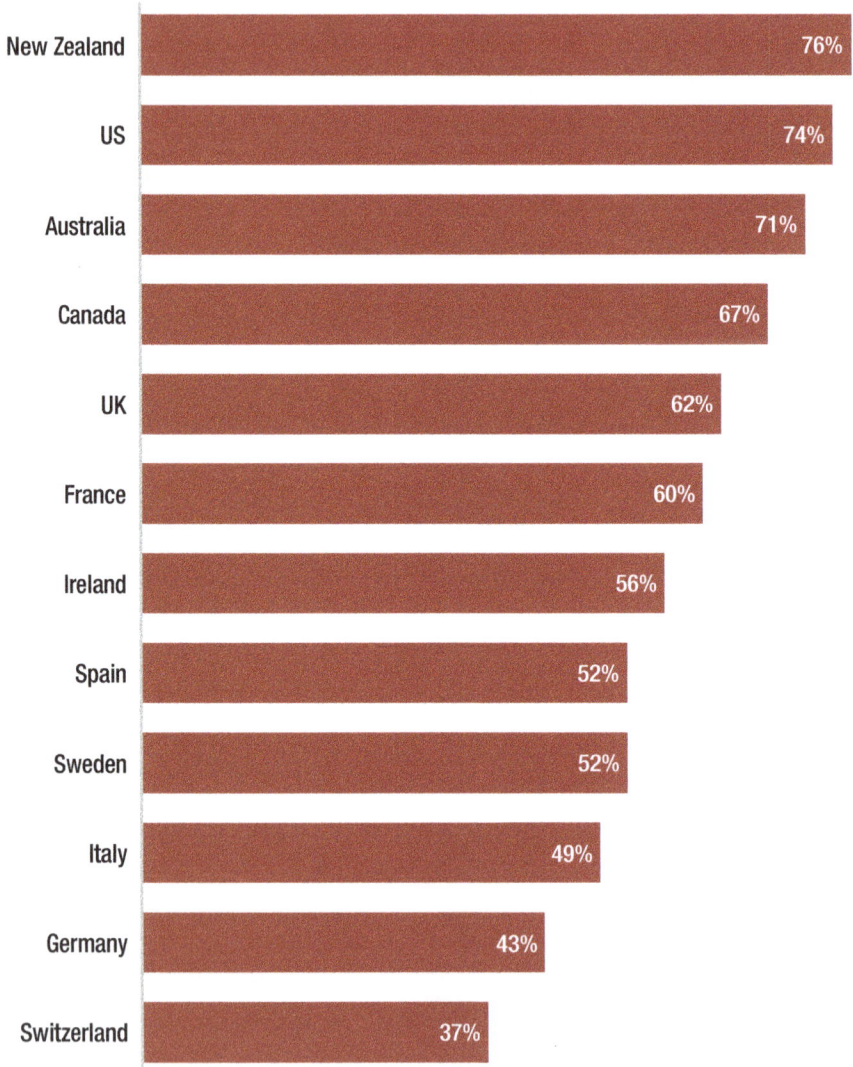

Country	Percent
New Zealand	76%
US	74%
Australia	71%
Canada	67%
UK	62%
France	60%
Ireland	56%
Spain	52%
Sweden	52%
Italy	49%
Germany	43%
Switzerland	37%

Base: Those attending church at least a few times a year.

GAPS AND GLIMPSES

There are many possible takeaways from a wide-ranging survey like this. Here are a few.

In many countries of the world, people have little or no familiarity with the Bible. This is especially true in places dominated, socially and/or politically, by non-Christian religions. Yet even in these areas, we see curiosity bubbling up. This report has focused on the Secular West, where the U.S. resides, historically and culturally. Here we find many people who have access to the Bible without any understanding of its value for their modern lives. Though the U.S. remains remarkably curious about both the Bible and Jesus, other Western nations seem to have lost the cultural ability and personal interest in discovering the timeless value of God's Word.

We're seeing a relevance gap. Yes, we know that sounds like a theme from a twentieth-century youth group, but the reality is crying out to us from these statistics. Outside of the U.S., when asked if the Bible is relevant to their lives, people are twice as likely to say no than yes. Those who want to learn about the Bible want help in relating the Bible to everyday life. A significant number said, "I do not think religion can be relevant to my life." Some church leaders "make the Bible relevant," but far from all. The relevance of Scripture will be established not with trendy buzzwords but by showing how God speaks into the issues of people's lives.

Americans are more committed to the Bible and Christian faith than others in the Secular West. To be sure, secularism is doing the same eroding in the U.S. as elsewhere, but that process seems further along in the other countries of Cluster 5. Here's a crucial question: Are the statistics from the rest of the Secular West a glimpse of America's future or a cautionary tale of decline that can be avoided? Also, how can American Christians advocate for the Bible at home and around the world, particularly helping others in our cluster of nations to re-engage with Scripture?

If we aspire to be "global Christians," spreading the message of Jesus to "the ends of the earth" (Acts 1:8), these data points will fuel our prayers and our ministry. The Patmos Initiative has given the world-wide church a great gift of information. We gain a greater understanding of the people we share this planet with—and in particular how open or closed they are to God's invitation in Scripture. ▪

PODCAST IN MAY: THE REBIRTH OF BELIEF

To better understand the state of the Bible around the world, we interviewed two guests for the *State of the Bible Podcast*.

First, **Justin Brierley**, based in the United Kingdom and author of *The Surprising Rebirth of Belief in God*, shares his perspective on what is happening in the Secular West.

Second, **Rhiannon McAleer**, Director of Research and Impact at the British and Foreign Bible Society, shares key takeaways from the *Patmos World Bible Attitudes Survey*.

State of the Bible
THE PODCAST

AMERICAN BIBLE SOCIETY

The Bible Around the World

5 BILLION+
copies of the Bible have been distributed worldwide

translated into

4,000
languages, in whole or in part

35%
of people around the world are interested in learning more about the Bible

7 in 10
(71%) agree it's good for children to know stories from the Bible

Opportunity

76%
of people in Asia say they know nothing about the Bible and

56%
have never even heard of it

Fewer than

4 in 10
residents (37%) in the "Secular West" countries believe the Bible is personally relevant to them

42% of Christians use the Bible weekly or more

37% use it less regularly

21% of Christians never use it

In partnership with the British and Foreign Bible Society and United Bible Societies, and with the expertise of the Gallup organization, the *Patmos World Bible Attitudes Survey* polled 91,000 people in 85 countries on Bible attitudes and practices.

HUMAN FLOURISHING

What does it mean to flourish? Not just to survive, but to thrive. The word suggests the blooming of a flower. Perhaps you've known times when you were trudging through life, one foot in front of the other, just existing—and other times when you have blossomed. At times you might flourish in one area of life and not in others. If you are a parent, or a teacher, or a church leader, you probably recognize flourishing when you see it in others. What can you do to encourage more of that?

Scholars at Harvard University have been studying human flourishing for nearly a decade. They define it as "the relative attainment of a state in which all aspects of a person's life are good, including the contexts in which that person lives."[1] Since 2017 they have collected data on six distinct ways in which people flourish.

---

1 VanderWeele, T.J., Johnson, B.R., Bialowolski, P.T. et al. The Global Flourishing Study: Study Profile and Initial Results on Flourishing. *Nat. Mental Health* (2025). https://doi.org/10.1038/s44220-025-00423-5

- Happiness & Life Satisfaction
- Mental & Physical Health
- Meaning & Purpose
- Character & Virtue
- Close Social Relationships
- Financial & Material Stability

The Human Flourishing Index gathers scores of 0 to 10 in each of these six domains and combines them into an overall flourishing score. (Actually, there are two overall scores. The Human Flourishing Index leaves out the financial domain, while the Secure Flourishing Index includes it.)

Since 2020, the *State of the Bible* survey has, with permission, included these Human Flourishing questions. Responses have consistently revealed a dramatic connection between flourishing and faith—especially Bible engagement and church involvement. We will unpack our most recent findings later in this chapter.

Meanwhile, the creators of the Human Flourishing Index have been working on a larger, more ambitious project—taking the survey international. This spring they announced the initial results of their Global Flourishing Study (GFS), with data from 22 nations of the world. In an event celebrating the GFS release, Tyler VanderWeele, an architect of the project, made a surprising connection. "One of the most consistent results across countries . . . is that participation in religious community is strongly associated with flourishing. Those who are attending services more than weekly report higher levels of flourishing." He listed additional data points about the value of "participation in a religious community"—lower rates of depression and suicide; greater social connection, marital stability, civic participation, charitable giving.

His question rang through this room of researchers, social work executives, and leaders in international development: *"Have we perhaps been neglecting important spiritual pathways to flourishing?"*[2]

FLOURISHING IN AMERICA AND THE WORLD

Before we get into the details of our own survey results on Human Flourishing in the U.S., let's see what Harvard's GFS says about how America stacks up globally.

The U.S. is not in the top half of the 22 nations in the Global Flourishing Study—either in the Human Flourishing metric or the Secure Flourishing metric, which includes a question on financial stability. Americans come in fifteenth in Human Flourishing; financial stability raises our Secure Flourishing position to twelfth.

The top four countries in both of those measures are Indonesia (by far the highest-scoring in both), Mexico, the Philippines, and Israel. Japan holds the lowest position, by far, in both, with the United Kingdom and Turkey also in the bottom three.

---

2 Tyler J. VanderWeele, remarks at the conference "The Global Flourishing Study: Exploring the Science and Meaning of Human Flourishing," April 30, 2025, Washington, DC (recorded at https://www.youtube.com/watch?v=HFoIbJceY7E).

Rankings of Nations in Human Flourishing and Secure Flourishing

Source: Global Flourishing Study

	Human Flourishing	
1	Indonesia	8.47
2	Mexico	8.19
3	Philippines	8.11
4	Israel	8.00
5	Nigeria	7.83
6	Argentina	7.79
7	Kenya	7.77
8	Egypt	7.63
9	Poland	7.63
10	Brazil	7.63
11	Tanzania	7.48
12	India	7.43
13	South Africa	7.41
14	Spain	7.31
15	United States	7.18
16	Hong Kong	7.17
17	Germany	7.11
18	Sweden	7.04
19	Australia	7.02
20	United Kingdom	6.88
21	Turkey	6.59
22	Japan	5.91

	Secure Flourishing	
1	Indonesia	8.10
2	Israel	7.87
3	Philippines	7.71
4	Mexico	7.64
5	Poland	7.55
6	Nigeria	7.37
7	Egypt	7.32
8	Kenya	7.28
9	Tanzania	7.19
10	Argentina	7.14
11	Hong Kong	7.12
12	United States	7.11
13	Sweden	7.10
14	South Africa	7.07
15	Brazil	7.02
16	Australia	7.01
17	Germany	7.01
18	Spain	6.89
19	India	6.87
20	United Kingdom	6.79
21	Turkey	6.32
22	Japan	5.87

Mean scores, based on self-reporting on a scale of 1 to 10 in response to ten questions, which cover five domains (for Human Flourishing) and adding two more questions on financial & material stability for the Secure Flourishing score.[3]

3 For further information, see the entry for "Human Flourishing Index" in the Definitions section of this report, page 196.

Readers should not confuse the Global Flourishing Study with the *Patmos Survey* from the previous chapter. While the Gallup Organization conducted both surveys, they were commissioned by two different entities, with different purposes and subject matter. The *Patmos Survey* focuses on attitudes about the Bible; the GFS on a broader assessment of human life.

With that in mind, you might still be wondering how the U.S. fares on flourishing in comparison to other "Secular West" nations. On the Patmos questions relating to the Bible, Americans outpaced others in Western Europe and other English-speaking nations in most measures. How do we compare in this entirely different survey on flourishing?

While the overall U.S. ranking is unimpressive (at #15 of 22), most other "Secular West" countries are worse. Spain ranks just ahead of the U.S. in Human Flourishing, but Germany, Sweden, Australia, and the United Kingdom trail behind. When financial stability is added to the results, the U.S. leads this whole cluster, slightly edging out Sweden.

A quick glance through this parade of nations reveals that the richest are not the most flourishing. As VanderWeele reported, "Wealthier nations seem not to be doing as well on relationships, meaning, and character. These are important aspects of flourishing. Flourishing is not just reducible to health, life satisfaction, and financial security. The other more humanistic aspects of flourishing are important individually . . . and they are also important for societal flourishing. . . . If we are to take flourishing seriously—if we are to become truly capable of promoting it—we must acknowledge its multi-faceted nature and we must pursue together those things that lie at the deepest core of our human nature."[4]

Students of Scripture will be happy to see how this academic study confirms biblical teaching, which warns against putting our hope in material wealth (1 Timothy 6:17). In Proverbs we read, "Whoever trusts in his riches will fall, but the righteous will flourish like a green leaf" (Proverbs 11:28 ESV).

Now, we turn to our own *State of the Bible* survey, specifically looking for connections between flourishing and faith.

FLOURISHING YEAR OVER YEAR

Where were you when the world stopped? The COVID shutdown of 2020 will take its place in the American collection of life-changing moments—certainly not the sudden terror of 9/11, but a rolling realization that life was going to be different for a while.

The *State of the Bible* report took a statistical snapshot of that time. The Human Flourishing Index was still quite new when we arranged to use it in our 2020 survey, conducted that January, less than two months before the pandemic hit. That served as a helpful baseline as events unfolded. We decided to do an extra survey that June, as COVID shutdowns continued. As expected, flourishing scores were down—with the exception of the "Character & Virtue" domain, which held steady that June and shot upward in the next poll.

---

4 Tyler J. VanderWeele, email followup from the GFS announcement, May 6, 2025.

Human Flourishing Domains and
Secure Flourishing Domains, 2020–25

- ● Happiness & Life Satisfaction
- ● Mental & Physical Health
- ● Meaning & Purpose
- ● Character & Virtue
- ● Close Social Relationships
- ● Financial & Material Stability

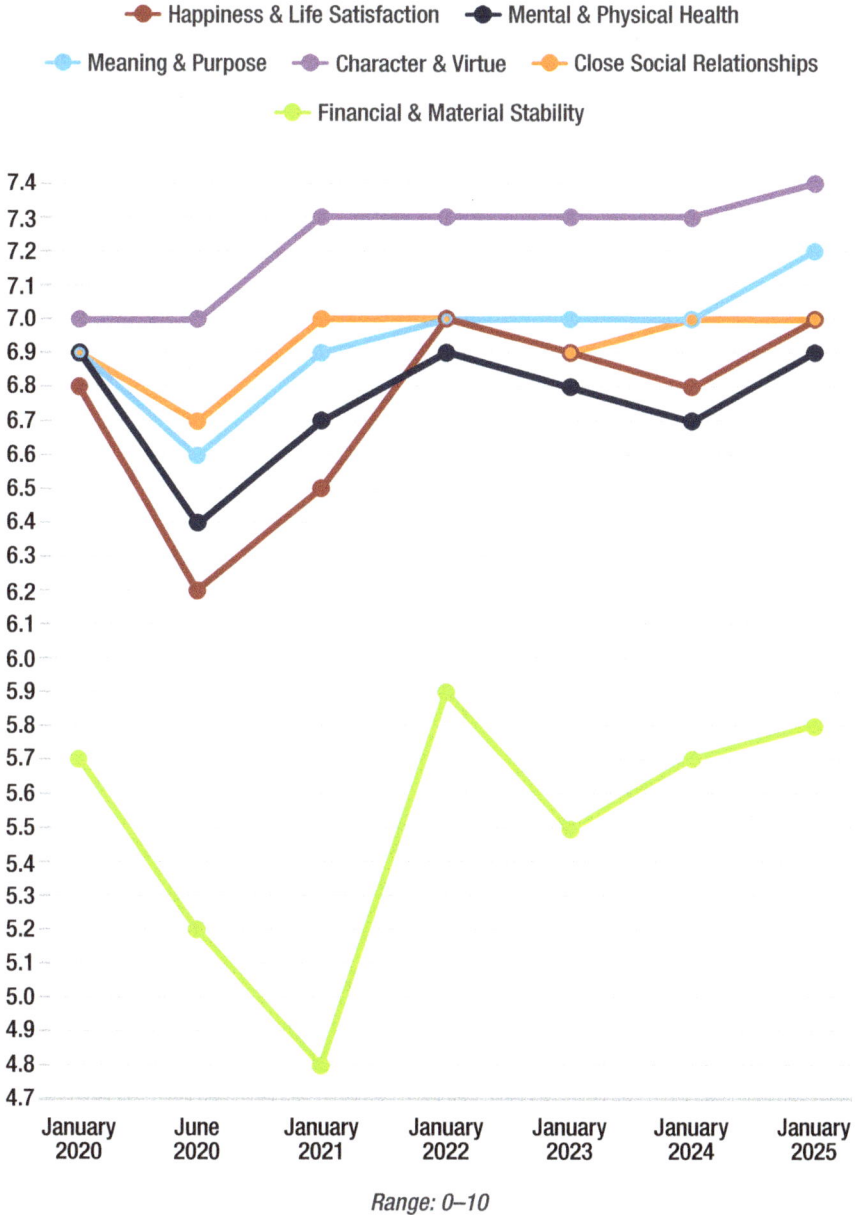

Range: 0–10

It took two years to return to the 2020 baseline, and we've seen slight dips and rises since. But this year's report shows a solid increase over last year across the board—up a tenth or two in every domain except "Close Social Relationships," which held steady. (That category has seen almost no vacillation since 2020.)

Human Flourishing and Secure Flourishing, 2020–25

Legend: Human Flourishing Index — Secure Flourishing Index

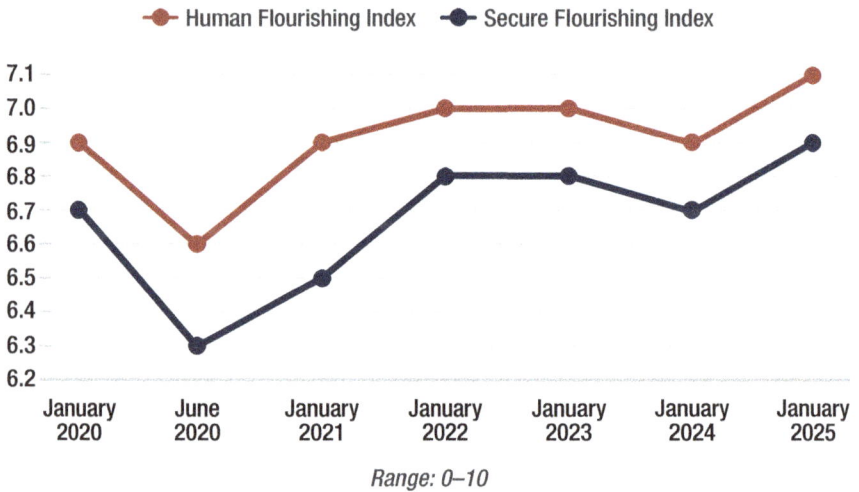

January 2020 | June 2020 | January 2021 | January 2022 | January 2023 | January 2024 | January 2025

Range: 0–10

DEMOGRAPHICS OF HUMAN FLOURISHING

The Boomer+ generation continues to have much higher flourishing scores than all younger **generations**. Generation Z has the lowest flourishing scores, but in most categories they're within a decimal or two of Millennials. "Happiness & Life Satisfaction" has the widest gap (Gen Z at 6.5, Millennials 6.8, Gen X 6.9). Surprisingly, the youngest group flourishes more in "Close Social Relationships," exceeding the scores of both middle generations. This is a reversal from previous years, when Gen Z trailed in the relationships category.

The two questions that make up the "Close Social Relationships" score are:

- *I am content with my friendships and relationships.*
- *My relationships are as satisfying as I would want them to be.*

Generations and Flourishing, Selected Categories

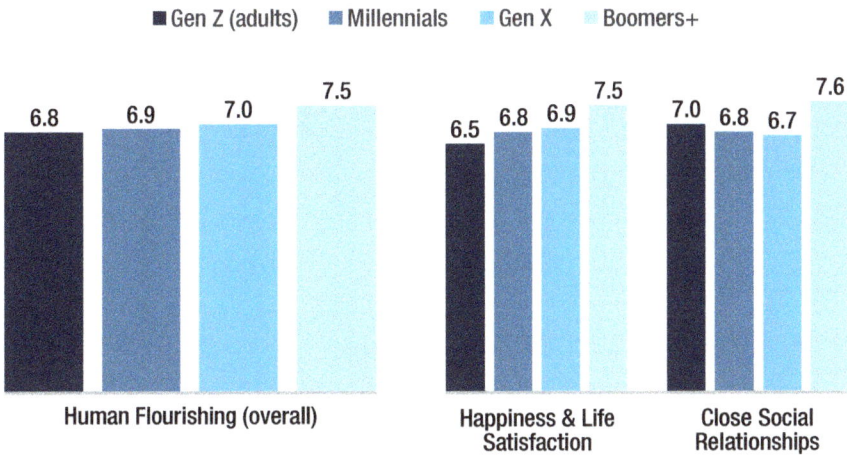

■ Gen Z (adults) ■ Millennials ■ Gen X ■ Boomers+

Human Flourishing (overall)

- 6.8 — Gen Z (adults)
- 6.9 — Millennials
- 7.0 — Gen X
- 7.5 — Boomers+

Happiness & Life Satisfaction

- 6.5 — Gen Z (adults)
- 6.8 — Millennials
- 6.9 — Gen X
- 7.5 — Boomers+

Close Social Relationships

- 7.0 — Gen Z (adults)
- 6.8 — Millennials
- 6.7 — Gen X
- 7.6 — Boomers+

Close Social Relationships by Generation, 2023–25

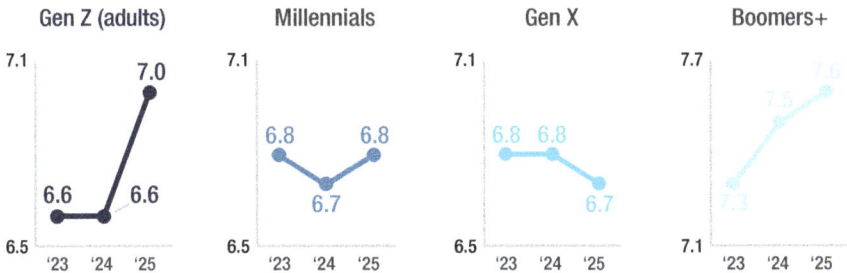

Gen Z (adults)
- 6.6 ('23)
- 6.6 ('24)
- 7.0 ('25)

Millennials
- 6.8 ('23)
- 6.7 ('24)
- 6.8 ('25)

Gen X
- 6.8 ('23)
- 6.8 ('24)
- 6.7 ('25)

Boomers+
- 7.3 ('23)
- 7.5 ('24)
- 7.6 ('25)

Range: 0–10

Most of the generational difference occurs in that second statement ("satisfying"). What has happened in the last year to make Gen Z relationships substantially more satisfying? In the last decade, scholars have highlighted the isolation and loneliness of Gen Z, often blaming the prevalence of smartphones. But here we find a blip of hope to counteract that assumption. Maybe some members of Gen Z are finding a "satisfying" balance in their connections within the real and virtual worlds. And here's another surprising detail. When we broke out the data for "Younger Gen Z" (ages 18–22) and Older Gen Z (23–28), the *younger* group scored significantly higher on Close Social Relationships (7.1 to 6.8). Does this simply reflect the difference between involvement in a college community (for many younger ones) and entry into an often-lonely workaday world (for many older ones), or is there a trend developing?

Education plays a major role in Human Flourishing. We know it generally leads to higher incomes, but even without the "Financial & Material Stability" category, people with Bachelor's degrees report significantly higher flourishing levels in all domains. Those with graduate degrees score even higher (Grad, 7.6 overall; Bachelor's, 7.3; lower levels, 6.9 and 7.0). There is little difference among those at lower educational levels, with or without a high school diploma, or even with some college.

Marital status clearly affects Human Flourishing, with married people scoring higher in every category than the never married. Those divorced, separated, or widowed have scores strewn in between.

Gender differences are minimal in most domains, but in every generation, men report significantly greater Financial & Material Stability than women (male 5.9; female 5.6).

Financial & Material Stability by Gender and Generation

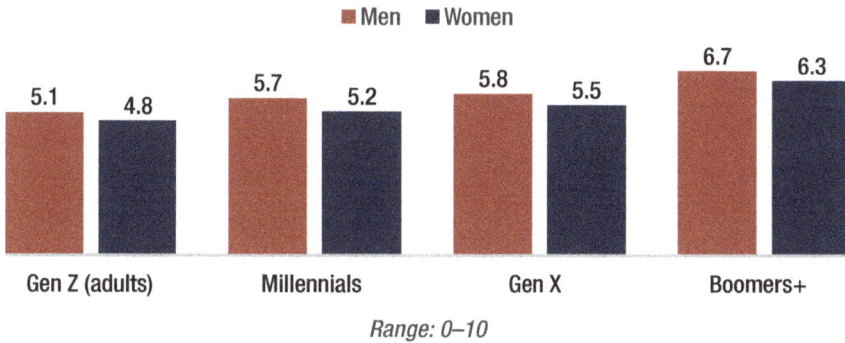

■ Men ■ Women

	Gen Z (adults)	Millennials	Gen X	Boomers+
Men	5.1	5.7	5.8	6.7
Women	4.8	5.2	5.5	6.3

Range: 0–10

FAITH AND HUMAN FLOURISHING

Personal practices of devotion are strongly associated with Human Flourishing.

Our survey asked people about various activities they had done "in the last seven days." Those who had *prayed to God, meditated, or volunteered in their community* reported much higher levels of Human Flourishing than those who had not.[5]

- People who have prayed in the past week are far more likely to flourish (39% reporting high Human Flourishing scores, compared with only 25% of those who haven't prayed).

5 On the self-reported scale of 1 to 10, High levels of Human Flourishing are scores of 8–10; Moderate levels are greater than 6 and less than 8; Low levels are 6 and under.

- People who have meditated in the past week are also far more likely to flourish (42% reporting high Human Flourishing scores, compared with only 29% of those who haven't meditated).
- People who have volunteered in their community are also far more likely to flourish (49% reporting high Human Flourishing scores, compared with only 30% of those who haven't volunteered).

Our readers will quickly observe that these practices are not necessarily Christian. Many Christians do these things as expressions of their faith, but many others do them as well. These findings suggest that there is something healthy about reaching outward, inward, or upward.

Levels of Human Flourishing by Practices

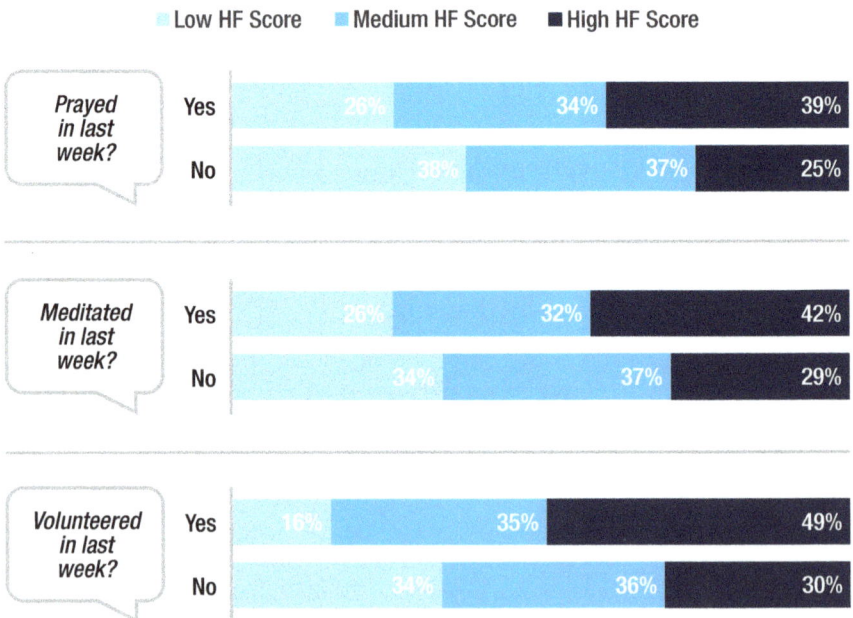

Low HF Score   Medium HF Score   High HF Score

Prayed in last week?
- Yes: 26% | 34% | 39%
- No: 38% | 37% | 25%

Meditated in last week?
- Yes: 26% | 32% | 42%
- No: 34% | 37% | 29%

Volunteered in last week?
- Yes: 16% | 35% | 49%
- No: 34% | 36% | 30%

But let's dig deeper into that matter of "reaching upward." Elsewhere in our survey, we ask self-identified Christians if they agree with the statement "God is active in my life." Consider what this statement is saying, and think about the Christians you know who might have trouble with it. They might recognize the *existence* of a God and even launch an occasional prayer, but this statement marks a move toward *involvement*, perhaps even a personal relationship.

In that light, it's no surprise to see the same pattern emerging. Those who agree with the statement are more likely to have high flourishing scores. And the more strongly they agree, the higher their flourishing levels.

Levels of Human Flourishing by Belief in God's Activity

"I believe God is actively involved in my life."

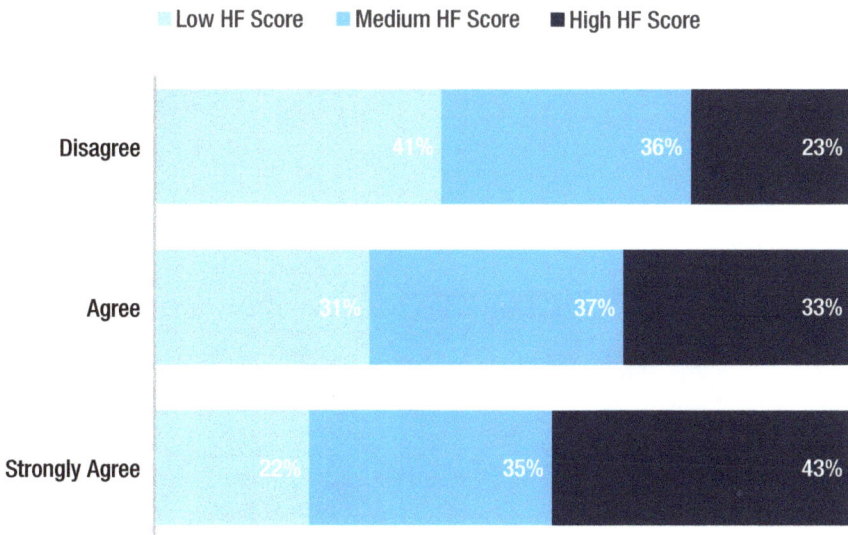

■ Low HF Score ■ Medium HF Score ■ High HF Score

	Low HF Score	Medium HF Score	High HF Score
Disagree	41%	36%	23%
Agree	31%	37%	33%
Strongly Agree	22%	35%	43%

Base: Self-identified Christians

How much does a person's church experience affect their flourishing? Considerably.

Last year we introduced the Faith Participation category, dividing people into four groups. **Practicing Christians** attend services at least once a month and say their faith is very important to them. **Casual Christians** attend at least monthly but don't say their faith is very important. **Nominal Christians** do not attend that often. **Non-Christians** do not call themselves Christians.

In Human Flourishing scores, we see a slight increase from Non-Christians to Nominal Christians (6.8 to 7.0), and another slight rise for Casual Christians (7.2). Then there's a huge jump to the Practicing Christian score (7.9). Church attendance, together with faith importance, is associated with greater flourishing.

Human Flourishing by Faith Participation

Faith Participation	Human Flourishing Score
Non-Christian	6.8
Nominal Christian	7.0
Casual Christian	7.2
Practicing Christian	7.9

Range: 0–10

BIBLE USE

Now we come to the main focus of the *State of the Bible* report: the Bible. Do people who regularly and meaningfully interact with Scripture report greater human flourishing?

Yes, clearly yes, and there are some fascinating details.

Every year, we ask not only *whether* people use the Bible, but *how often*. We know that God meets people in Scripture whenever they turn to it, whether daily or weekly or just on special occasions. But over the years we've observed that the frequency of people's Bible use says something about their connection with God. Those who come to Scripture just a few times a year have a certain place in their lives for the Bible—maybe as a blessing for the holidays. Those who read once a week may have a different pattern, perhaps a Sabbath blessing or other weekly ritual. But more frequent Bible use—several times a week or more—nurtures spiritual growth and intimacy with God in a day-to-day way. As people grow, they want to dig into the Bible more, and as they meet God in those pages, they keep growing.

The Human Flourishing data give us statistical confirmation of the biblical idea that God's Word is good for you. We clearly see that greater levels of personal Bible Use are associated with higher Human Flourishing scores. But there's not much difference between using the Bible once a week (7.2) and "three or four times a year" (7.1). The major impact on flourishing begins when you get beyond the "once a week" level of Bible use. A jump to "several times a week" raises the flourishing level by three decimal points (to 7.5), and daily use has an even higher jump (to 7.9).

Human Flourishing Scores by Bible Use Frequency

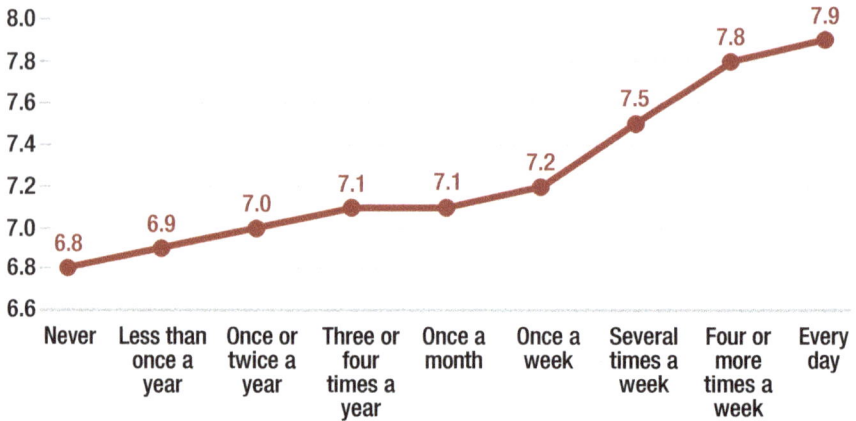

Frequency	Score
Never	6.8
Less than once a year	6.9
Once or twice a year	7.0
Three or four times a year	7.1
Once a month	7.1
Once a week	7.2
Several times a week	7.5
Four or more times a week	7.8
Every day	7.9

Personal Bible Use; Range: 0–10

We want to be careful about assuming causality. That is, the numbers themselves just give us *association*. Greater flourishing goes together with more frequent Bible use. Perhaps those who flourish in character, relationships, and mental and physical health have the personal discipline and drive to develop a Bible-reading habit. Maybe such discipline leads to both Bible use and aspects of flourishing.

But we're also very aware of how God changes lives through the Bible. And the Bible tells us this again and again. As the Psalmist sings:

The Law of the LORD is perfect;
   it gives us new life.
His teachings last forever,
and they give wisdom
   to ordinary people.

The LORD's instruction is right;
   it makes our hearts glad.
His commands shine brightly,
   and they give us light.

Psalm 19:7–8 CEV

SCRIPTURE ENGAGEMENT

Frequency of Bible Use is one piece of our definition of measurable Scripture Engagement, which also includes responses to questions about the impact of Scripture on our relationship with God and others and the centrality of Scripture in our decision-making. As we reported in chapter 1, only one in five Americans (20%) are Scripture Engaged. As a group, these people flourish more (7.9) than those who don't share that connection with the Bible (7.0 for Movable Middle and 6.8 for Bible Disengaged).

Human Flourishing Scores by Scripture Engagement

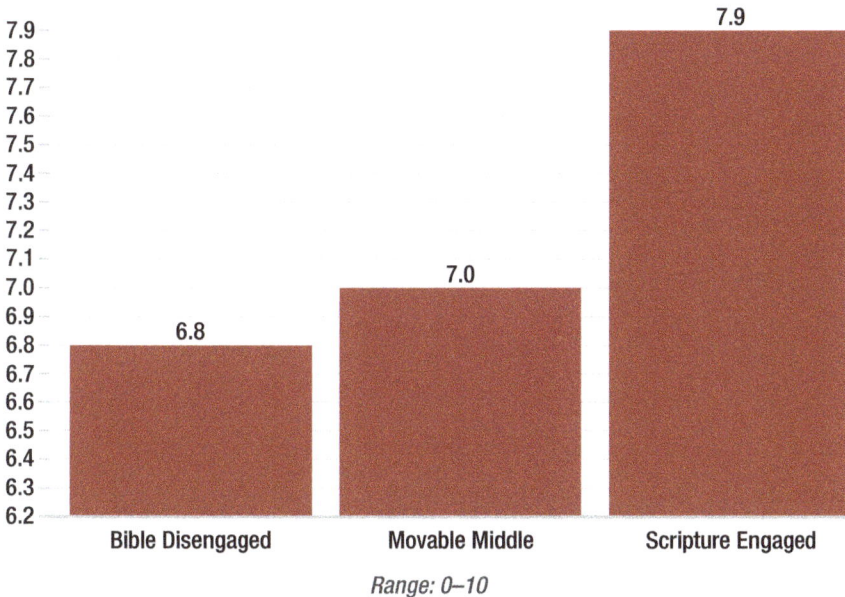

Range: 0–10

The Scripture Engaged have higher scores in every one of the five Human Flourishing domains, but the greatest difference occurs in Meaning & Purpose, where they have an increase of 22 percent over the Bible Disengaged. It's easy to see how the call of Scripture to a deeper relationship with God and service to others would create a powerful sense of purpose in those who regularly peruse those pages.

Earlier we saw that the two youngest generations have the lowest levels of flourishing, but when we add Scripture engagement into the equation, we see something different. Both Gen Zers and Millennials who are Scripture engaged have an average Human Flourishing score of 8.1! We've seen this generational effect in past years, too. Young people who are Scripture engaged appear to be truly thriving.

The only domain where the Bible Disengaged excel is the sixth one, which is added to create the Secure Flourishing Index. In that Financial & Material Stability domain, the Bible Disengaged have a score of 6.0, significantly above the Scripture Engaged (5.7) and the Movable Middle (5.3). The questions for this domain are not about income or wealth, but about how much people *worry* about meeting monthly expenses, or about safety, food, or housing. Still, we can see how greater wealth might lead to less worry, and in fact the Bible Disengaged report higher income levels than the Scripture Engaged.

Selected Flourishing Domains by Scripture Engagement

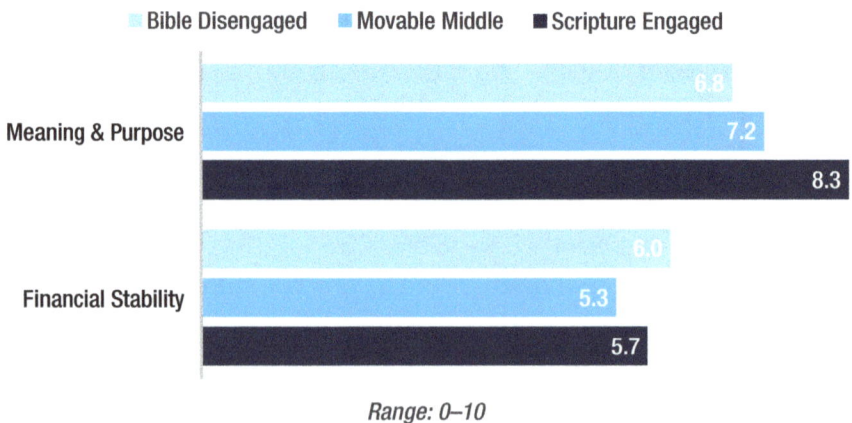

■ Bible Disengaged   ■ Movable Middle   ■ Scripture Engaged

Meaning & Purpose
- Bible Disengaged: 6.8
- Movable Middle: 7.2
- Scripture Engaged: 8.3

Financial Stability
- Bible Disengaged: 6.0
- Movable Middle: 5.3
- Scripture Engaged: 5.7

Range: 0–10

OTHER SPIRITUAL KEYS TO FLOURISHING

Imagine that someone in your church comes to you for advice. "I pray and read the Bible a lot," they say, "but I still don't feel that I'm *flourishing*." (They might not use that exact word, but you get the idea.) What do you tell them?

There are many reasons that Christians might not be flourishing, including some very serious matters. And there are many ways Christians might flourish more. But our survey discovered two practices that are statistically associated—clearly and strongly—with greater levels of flourishing.

Are they in a Bible study group? In one section of our survey, we asked Bible Users about methods of Bible reading—a few verses at a time or whole chapters, same time of day, and so on (see page 16). One yes/no option was "I participate in a Bible study group." About 22 percent said yes (which, by the way, is nearly one-tenth of the American population).

Those who participate in a Bible study group had an average Human Flourishing score of 7.9, far exceeding the national average in every domain. People who participate in a Bible study group also saw higher flourishing levels across every domain than those using any other Bible reading method.

If you want to start flourishing, you might tell your advisee, join a Bible study group. While that might sound simplistic, think about it. In a group, people can develop close social relationships. They share moments of joy and challenge, spiritual growth and learning opportunities, as the Spirit guides them through Scripture. They receive and offer important feedback on their life—including mental and physical health—based on biblical principles. They see what the Bible says about God's purposes, which might bolster their own sense of meaning and purpose. The group Bible study might even help them worry less about financial and material security, as they help each other and encourage one another to put their trust in God.

The Effect of a Bible Study Group on Flourishing

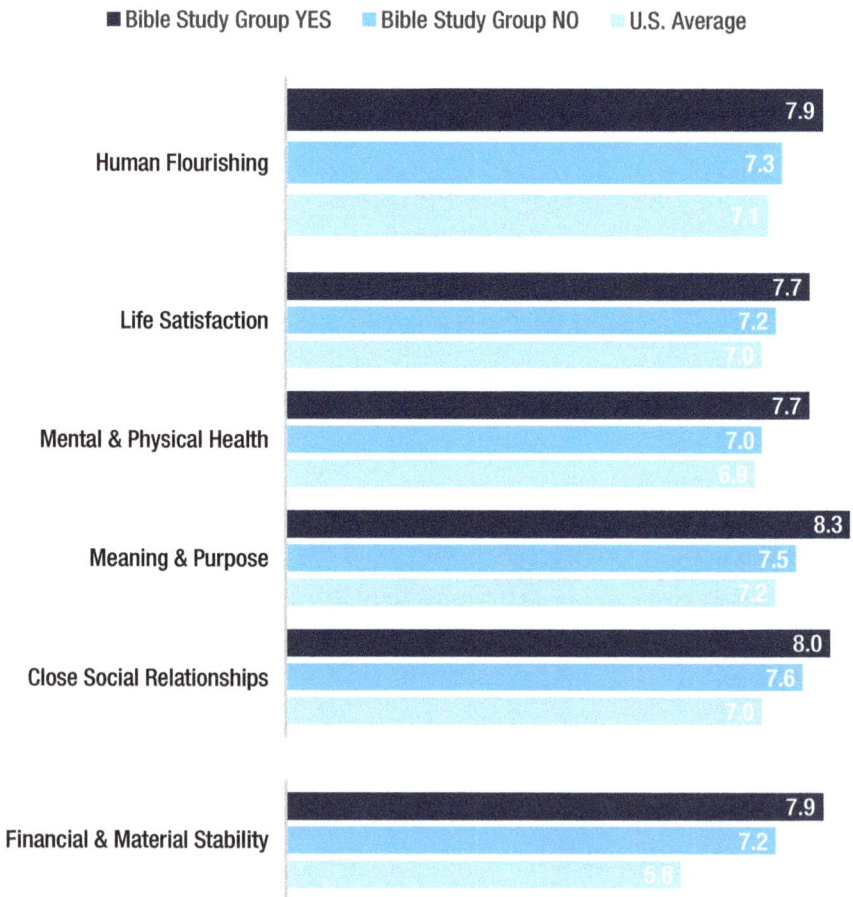

■ Bible Study Group YES ■ Bible Study Group NO ■ U.S. Average

Category	Bible Study Group YES	Bible Study Group NO	U.S. Average
Human Flourishing	7.9	7.3	7.1
Life Satisfaction	7.7	7.2	7.0
Mental & Physical Health	7.7	7.0	6.9
Meaning & Purpose	8.3	7.5	7.2
Close Social Relationships	8.0	7.6	7.0
Financial & Material Stability	7.9	7.2	6.8

Base: Bible Users; Range: 0–10

Are they using their spiritual gifts? In another portion of our survey we asked self-identified Christians if they agreed with this statement: *I know and use my spiritual gifts to fulfill God's purposes.* The more they agreed with this statement, the higher their Flourishing score. This was true across all domains, but the most dramatic results were in Meaning & Purpose.

This might, then, involve more than mere advice to this non-flourishing friend. You might need to make sure your church is identifying spiritual gifts and using them in ministry, helping members join with God's purposes for the church and community.

Human Flourishing and Spiritual Gifts

"I know and use my spiritual gifts to fulfill God's purposes."

■ Human Flourishing Score　　■ Meaning & Purpose Score

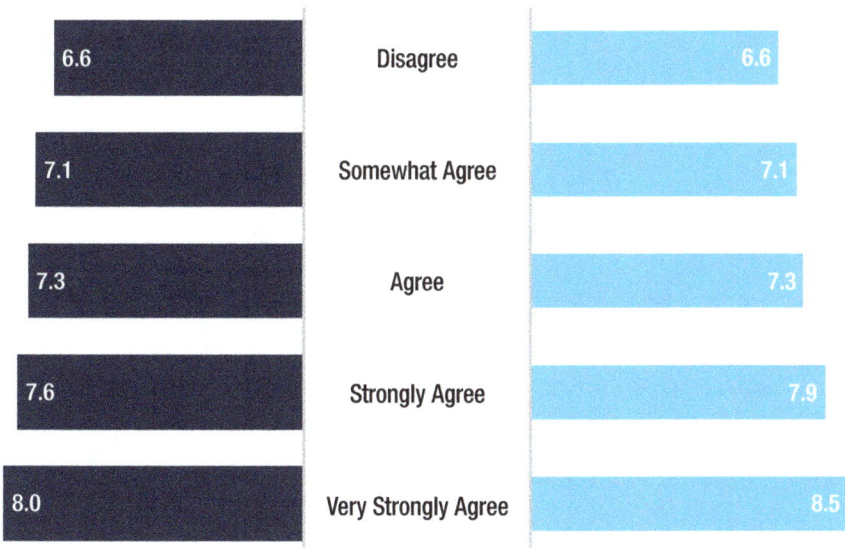

	Human Flourishing Score		Meaning & Purpose Score
Disagree	6.6		6.6
Somewhat Agree	7.1		7.1
Agree	7.3		7.3
Strongly Agree	7.6		7.9
Very Strongly Agree	8.0		8.5

Base: Self-identified Christians

Knowing God, loving God, letting God's love flow through us to others—these are our goals. We use our spiritual gifts, not to attain some level of success or happiness, but simply because the Lord wants us to. We study the Bible with others because Jesus said he'd be there when we gather in his name—and what a privilege it is to talk together about what the Lord reveals in Scripture!

Even flourishing is not an end in itself. It is a blessing God provides when we trust him and walk with him. Scripture often reminds us that our connection with God brings about abundant life, great joy, peace that passes understanding, rich blessing, and even *flourishing*. It's nice to see survey data confirming that. ◼

CHAPTER 3 PODCAST: THE CHURCH'S ROLE IN FLOURISHING

For this chapter, we interviewed **Dr. Kate Long**, a research associate with the Human Flourishing Program at Harvard University. She studies the intersection of faith and flourishing and brings a wealth of knowledge to the conversation. We hope you'll listen in!

Human Flourishing

Average American
Human Flourishing Score **7.1**

0 ——————————●————————— 10

Human Flourishing by Generation

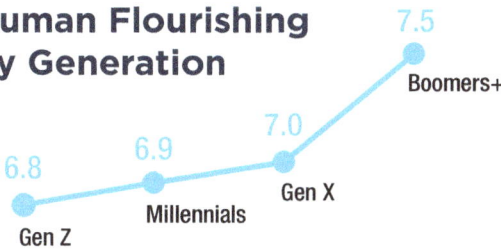

7.5
Boomers+

7.0
Gen X

6.9
Millennials

6.8
Gen Z

U.S. Human
Flourishing
Ranking:

#15

out of 22
countries
studied*

Global Flourishing Study (Harvard/Gallup 2025) | globalflourishingstudy.com

Faith and Flourishing

Flourishing increases with
Bible reading.

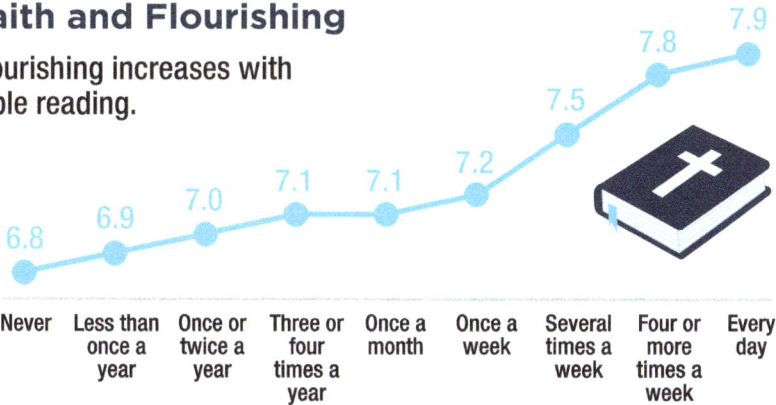

7.9 Every day
7.8 Four or more times a week
7.5 Several times a week
7.2 Once a week
7.1 Once a month
7.1 Three or four times a year
7.0 Once or twice a year
6.9 Less than once a year
6.8 Never

Never	Less than once a year	Once or twice a year	Three or four times a year	Once a month	Once a week	Several times a week	Four or more times a week	Every day
6.8	6.9	7.0	7.1	7.1	7.2	7.5	7.8	7.9

And Scripture-engaged Gen Z
& Millennials are flourishing:

8.1 Scripture Engaged

6.7 Unengaged
6.9 All

DEFINITION

Human flourishing: A state of thriving and
well-being where all aspects of a person's
life are good.

CHAPTER 4

SELF-CARE AND WELL-BEING

For years, Lester Holt signed off the NBC Nightly News by saying, "Please take care of yourself . . . and each other." Perhaps you have used "Take care of yourself" as a farewell to friends. Yet this is now more than a catchphrase. Self-care has become a hot topic in the health industry.

While researchers gather different behaviors under the self-care umbrella, there's a growing awareness that people can substantially improve their own mental, physical, and spiritual health with certain beneficial actions.

The *State of the Bible* survey includes questions on five specific self-care activities: **physical exercise, spending time with a friend, volunteering, meditation,** and **prayer**. We want to see whether these behaviors help people flourish and what effect they might have on people's stress, anxiety, or loneliness. Also, do Scripture Engaged people or Practicing Christians practice self-care more or less than others?

Even the academic studies on this subject are quick to point out that self-care does not mean selfishness or self-absorption, though some people could go to that extreme. We anchor this line of questioning in the biblical command to "love your neighbor *as yourself*" (Leviticus 19:18; Matthew 22:39)—and its assumption that we can care for both ourselves and others.

FIVE ACTIVITIES FOR SELF-CARE

Our question asks whether people have done these activities in the past week. Not whether they think it's a good idea, or if they'll get around to it when they get a chance, but simply . . .

Have you engaged in any of the following activities in the last seven days?

- Engaged in physical exercise
- Spent time with a friend (not a family member)
- Volunteered in my community
- Meditated
- Prayed to God

Self-Care Activities, U.S. Adults

Activity	Percentage
Physical Exercise	67%
Spend Time with a Friend	66%
Volunteer in my Community	17%
Meditate	35%
Pray to God	60%

About two of three people say they've exercised (67%) or spent time with a friend (66%) in the previous week. Volunteering seems more difficult, with only about one in six (17%) doing this. Praying to God (60%) is more common than meditating (35%).

Note that most of these activities are not necessarily Christian or even spiritual, but they could be. Someone might volunteer for a Christian ministry or for a Little League team. Someone might meditate on the goodness of God or on the height of their blood pressure. Keep that in mind as we look at the numbers for different subgroups.

GENERATION AND GENDER

You might be surprised at the lack of variation in physical exercise, with all four generations clustered around that two-thirds mark. It's also interesting that the oldest and youngest spend the most time with friends (about 10 percentage points higher than the middle generation groups). Volunteering is tough for everybody, it seems, and it looks like the retirees in our oldest generation are pushing that number up (to 23%, nine points higher than any other group).

Self-Care Activities by Generation

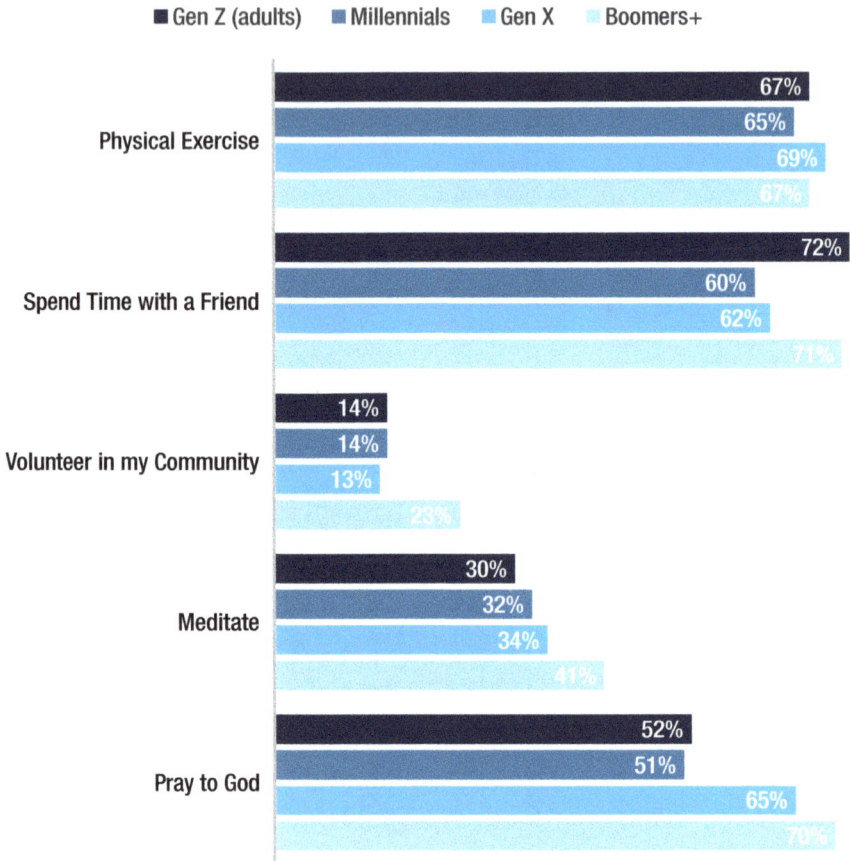

■ Gen Z (adults)　■ Millennials　■ Gen X　■ Boomers+

Physical Exercise
- 67%
- 65%
- 69%
- 67%

Spend Time with a Friend
- 72%
- 60%
- 62%
- 71%

Volunteer in my Community
- 14%
- 14%
- 13%
- 23%

Meditate
- 30%
- 32%
- 34%
- 41%

Pray to God
- 52%
- 51%
- 65%
- 70%

In the two spiritual, or at least quasi-spiritual, activities—prayer and meditation—we see the oldest generation (70%) outpacing the others again, though about two-thirds of Gen X (65%) had prayed in the previous week. It's possible that older people relate more to the term *meditate* than younger ones (the concept had a heyday back in the Seventies). Other studies show that younger generations especially appreciate God's presence in nature, but they might not call it meditation.

We also looked at gender differences with these Self-Care items. Women were slightly more likely to spend time with a friend (67% to 64%) or to volunteer in the community (18% to 15%). But the biggest shift occurred in the prayer numbers, with women far more likely than men to report praying to God in the previous seven days (65% to 57%).

FLOURISHING AND SELF-CARE

In Chapter 3, we discussed the Human Flourishing Index, with its six domains, examining various factors associated with greater flourishing. Now, as we turn to self-care and other issues, we wonder about their connection with flourishing. If people are truly "taking care of themselves" in these physical, social, emotional, and spiritual ways, shouldn't they have higher flourishing numbers?

High Flourishing by Self-Care Activities

Percent of those doing (or not doing) these activities who have high Human Flourishing levels

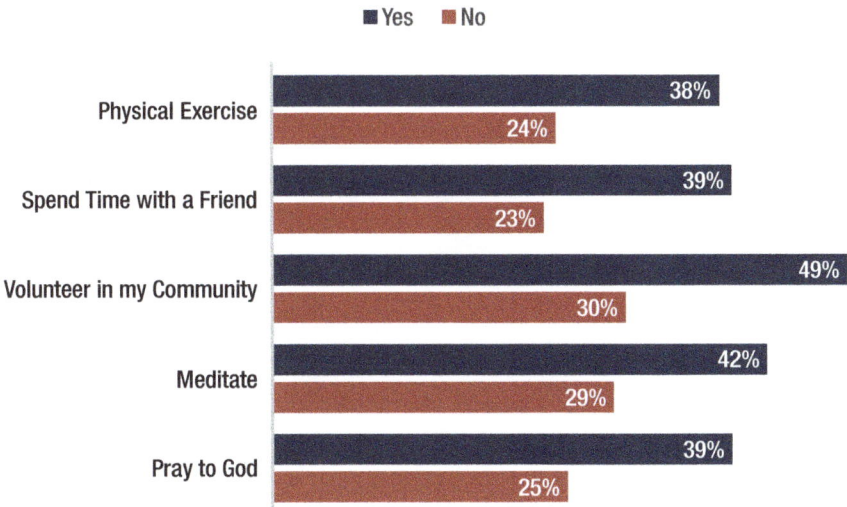

■ Yes ■ No

Activity	Yes	No
Physical Exercise	38%	24%
Spend Time with a Friend	39%	23%
Volunteer in my Community	49%	30%
Meditate	42%	29%
Pray to God	39%	25%

We designate index scores of 8.0 and above as "high flourishing." So we hypothesized that those who engaged in our five Self-Care activities would have significantly more "high flourishers" than those who did not engage in those activities. That's exactly what we found.

With each of the five Self-Care activities, participation makes for a difference of at least 13 percentage points in the number of high-flourishing people. We find the greatest difference (49% to 30%) in the Volunteering numbers. This is likely because volunteers are far more likely to be Scripture Engaged, Practicing Christians, and in the Boomer+ generation—all factors associated with higher levels of flourishing.

Breaking out the different domains in the Human Flourishing Index that reflect various parts of our lives, it is clear that some domains match up well with Self-Care activities we asked about. For instance, we figured that those who had exercised physically in the previous week might feel better about their Physical & Mental Health. Those who have spent time with a friend might be flourishing more in their Close Social Relationships. Once again, that's exactly what we found.

You might intuitively expect that those who pray to God regularly would have a greater sense of Meaning & Purpose, and they do. Same with those who meditate. Those who volunteer in the community had the greatest difference over non-volunteers in two domains—Meaning & Purpose and Close Social Relationships—which makes make sense in both cases. Volunteers often enjoy making a difference in the world, and they might make friends among those who volunteer alongside them.

Increase in Flourishing Domains
for Self-Care Activities

■ Human Flourishing Score for "No"   ■ Human Flourishing Score for "Yes"

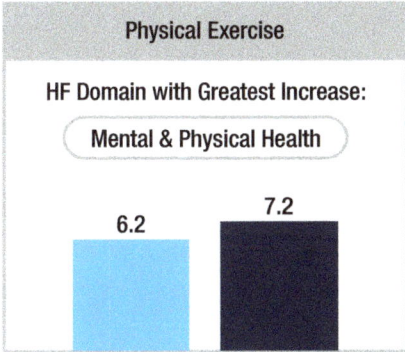

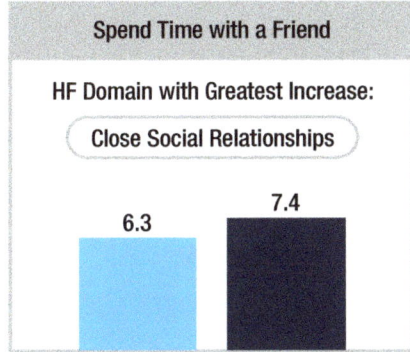

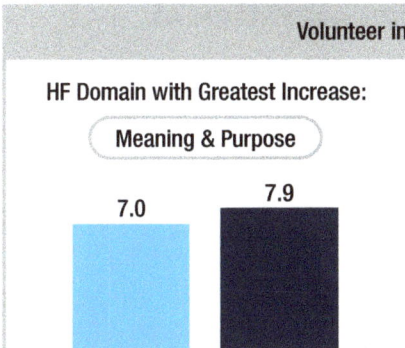

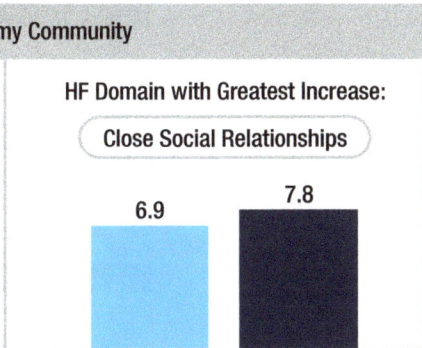

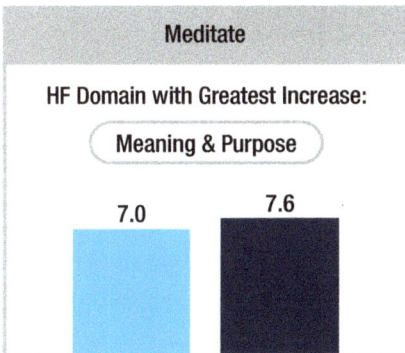

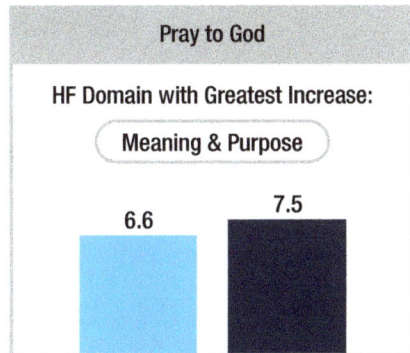

Physical Exercise

HF Domain with Greatest Increase:

Mental & Physical Health

6.2   7.2

Spend Time with a Friend

HF Domain with Greatest Increase:

Close Social Relationships

6.3   7.4

Volunteer in my Community

HF Domain with Greatest Increase:

Meaning & Purpose

7.0   7.9

HF Domain with Greatest Increase:

Close Social Relationships

6.9   7.8

Meditate

HF Domain with Greatest Increase:

Meaning & Purpose

7.0   7.6

Pray to God

HF Domain with Greatest Increase:

Meaning & Purpose

6.6   7.5

SELF-CARE AND FAITH

As we've noted, most of these Self-Care activities could be considered expressions of a believer's spiritual life. Even if not explicitly spiritual, these behaviors might be considered "faith-adjacent." So how do the most seriously committed Christians fare? Are they more likely to engage in these practices?

Self-Care Activities by Scripture Engagement

Percent reporting that they've done this in the previous seven days

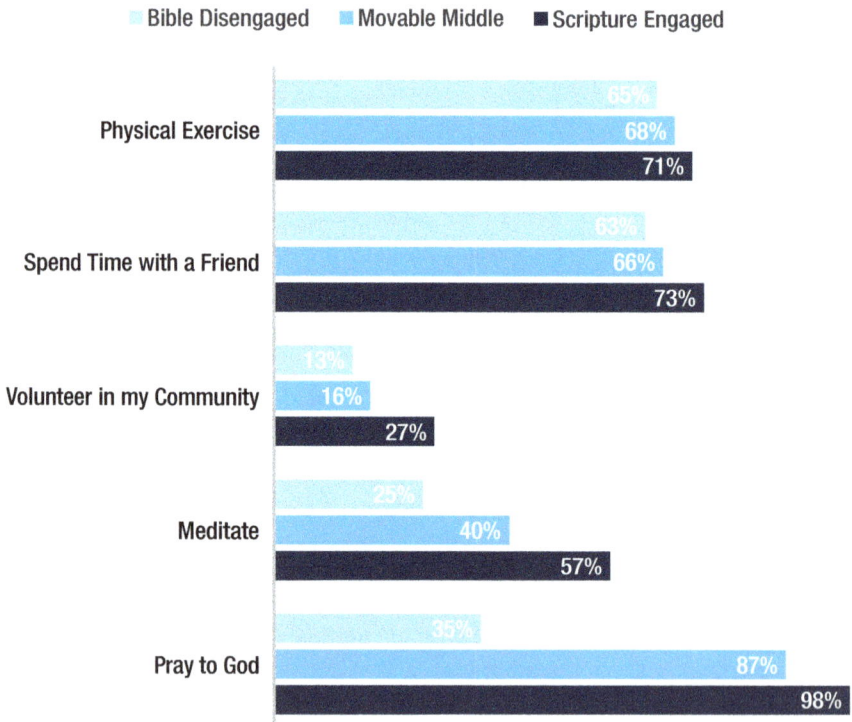

Bible Disengaged Movable Middle Scripture Engaged

Activity	Bible Disengaged	Movable Middle	Scripture Engaged
Physical Exercise	65%	68%	71%
Spend Time with a Friend	63%	66%	73%
Volunteer in my Community	13%	16%	27%
Meditate	25%	40%	57%
Pray to God	35%	87%	98%

Scripture Engaged people practice *all* these activities at a higher rate, though their margin is slim in the Physical Exercise category (71%, compared to 68% and 65%). There, we wonder if the greater discipline necessary for regular engagement with Scripture carries over into physical fitness, providing a slight edge. Similarly, the Scripture Engaged are more likely to spend time with a friend (73% to 66% and 63%). Many people spend time with friends, regardless of their relationship with Scripture, but these numbers suggest that the Bible might provide an extra push. (Scripture Engaged people also tend to be churchgoing people, which may enhance their relational options.)

We see that "extra push" most clearly in the volunteering category, where the Scripture Engaged far exceed others (27% to 16% and 13%). Keep in mind that this is volunteering "in my community" and includes people who volunteer in their local church.

You could predict that the Scripture Engaged would far exceed the others in Meditation and Prayer, but keep your eye on the Movable Middle. They're *moving*. In other activities they've been only a few percentage points away from the Bible Disengaged. They begin to create some space in Meditation (40% Movable Middle to 25% Disengaged), and when it comes to Praying to God, they're nearly at the level of the Scripture Engaged (87% to 98%).

We have long presented the Movable Middle as a "sleeping giant" of Christian ministry. They are less committed in many ways, but they have some mustard seed of faith, and we see it in these numbers. In any given week, nearly nine of ten of them are "praying to God." We don't know why, or what they're saying, but we know that's a relationship we want to encourage.

Many of the Movable Middle are also part of a group we used to call Non-Practicing Christians. Last year we sliced this group into two very different subgroups. **Nominal Christians** say they're Christians but rarely attend church. **Casual Christians** attend church but do not say their faith is "very important" to them.

The difference between Nominals and Casuals becomes apparent as we view their Self-Care activities. Casual Christians are very close the Practicing Christians in most points, sometimes exceeding them. Nominal Christians lag behind Non-Christians in everything except prayer.

Self-Care Activities by Faith Participation

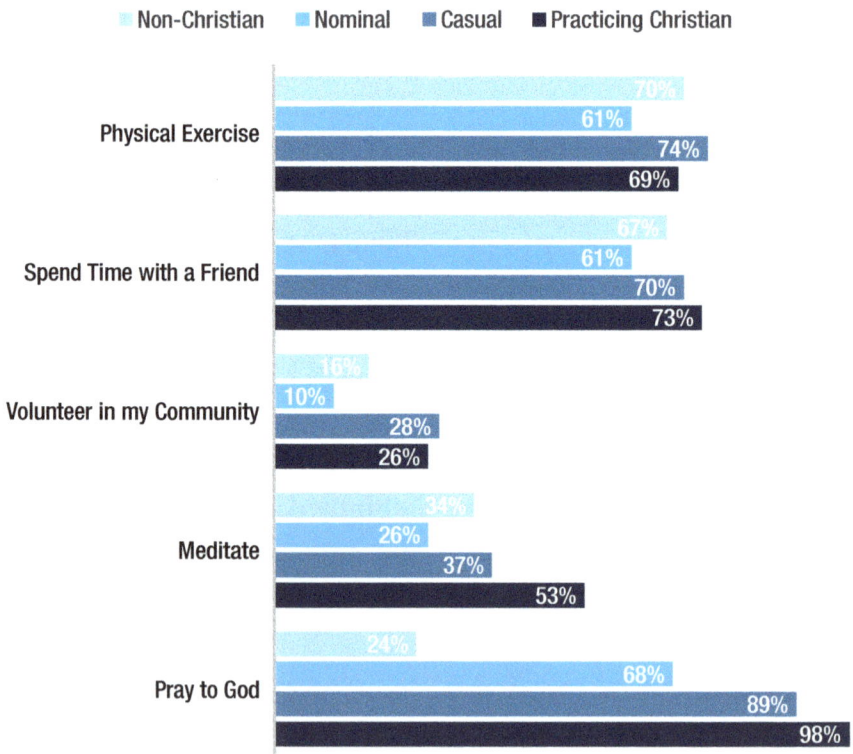

Non-Christian ■ Nominal ■ Casual ■ Practicing Christian

Physical Exercise
- 70%
- 61%
- 74%
- 69%

Spend Time with a Friend
- 67%
- 61%
- 70%
- 73%

Volunteer in my Community
- 16%
- 10%
- 28%
- 26%

Meditate
- 34%
- 26%
- 37%
- 53%

Pray to God
- 24%
- 68%
- 89%
- 98%

FOUR FACTORS RELATING TO WELL-BEING

Despite our best efforts in self-care, we can face obstacles to well-being. We feel **stress** from work demands, family concerns, financial challenges, or national issues. Occasionally this stress overflows into a general feeling of **anxiety.** Sometimes we find that the comfort of friends eases our concerns, but at other times we experience **loneliness**, convinced that no one truly understands us or cares.

Our researchers recognize that stress, anxiety, or loneliness can become serious issues, requiring medical attention and professional counseling. We also know that there are lower levels of these ailments that can still affect our health, attitudes, and quality of life. We're not doing any diagnoses here, just asking how people feel. A bank of questions on these subjects yields scores that we can compare from group to group. We also include a few questions gauging the **hope** level of our respondents. Well-being isn't just the reduction of negative feelings, but also a positive attitude toward the future.

That brings us to the Self-Care activities we just discussed. Do they actually help with stress and these other issues? While there may be other factors involved, these activities are consistently associated with lower stress and anxiety, less loneliness, and more hope.[1]

The stress-reducing power of physical exercise is well-established, and our data confirm it. Yet it's also associated with less loneliness and more hope. The most important element on that chart might be the dismal numbers for those who *don't* exercise.

---

1 These Well-Being items use different scales based on self-reporting in answer to questions on our survey. Stress has a scale of 0–40; Anxiety is 0–20; Loneliness is 5–20 (lower is better for all three). Hope is 3–24 (higher is better).

The Effect of Physical Exercise on Well-Being Issues

Have you engaged in physical exercise in the last seven days?

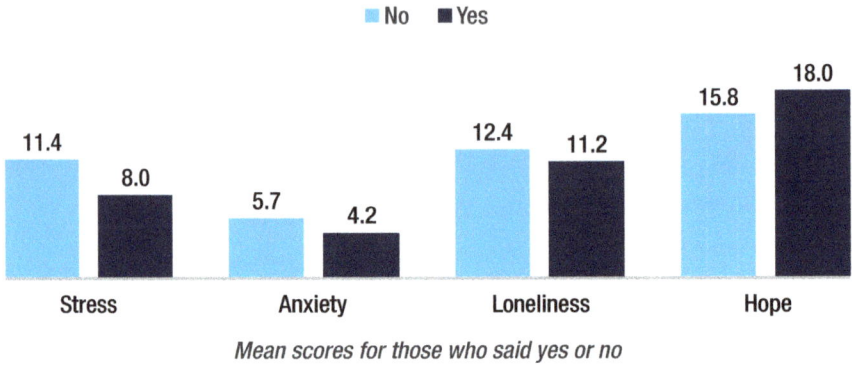

■ No ■ Yes

	Stress	Anxiety	Loneliness	Hope
No	11.4	5.7	12.4	15.8
Yes	8.0	4.2	11.2	18.0

Mean scores for those who said yes or no

The Effect of Time Spent with a Friend on Well-Being Issues

Have you spent time with a friend (not family) in the last seven days?

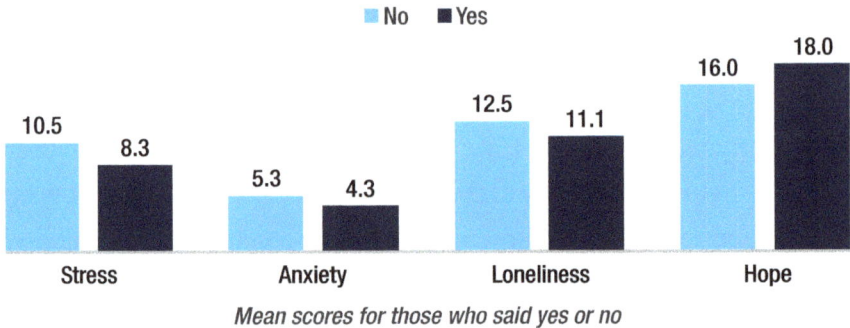

■ No ■ Yes

	Stress	Anxiety	Loneliness	Hope
No	10.5	5.3	12.5	16.0
Yes	8.3	4.3	11.1	18.0

Mean scores for those who said yes or no

The relatively few (17%) who volunteer in their communities put up the most positive numbers. They are the least stressed, least anxious, least lonely, and most hopeful of everyone represented on these charts. (Again, volunteers are also far more likely to come from the Boomer+ generation, which shows better scores in the Well-Being categories, so this may skew the data somewhat.)

The Effect of Volunteering on Well-Being Issues

Have you volunteered in your community in the last seven days?

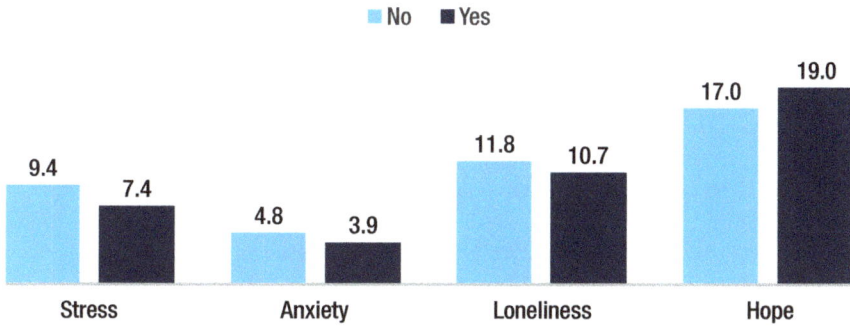

■ No ■ Yes

	Stress	Anxiety	Loneliness	Hope
No	9.4	4.8	11.8	17.0
Yes	7.4	3.9	10.7	19.0

Mean scores for those who said yes or no

The spiritual act of prayer and the social act of spending time with a friend are also associated with greater well-being across the board. On the other hand, meditation showed minimal difference. Those who meditated in the previous week actually reported slightly *more* anxiety. We should note here that these questions don't determine causation. Perhaps anxiety causes people to meditate.

The Effect of Meditation on Well-Being Issues

Have you meditated in the last seven days?

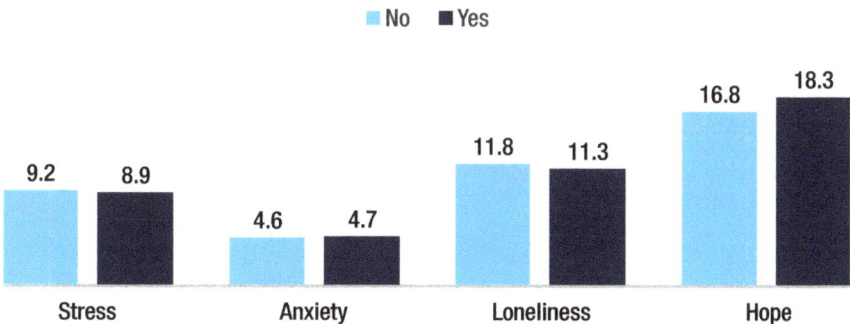

■ No ■ Yes

	Stress	Anxiety	Loneliness	Hope
No	9.2	4.6	11.8	16.8
Yes	8.9	4.7	11.3	18.3

Mean scores for those who said yes or no

This may be true of prayer as well, which shows less of a Yes/No difference than exercising, volunteering, or time with a friend. While we believe that prayer can reduce stress, anxiety, and loneliness, we also understand that people in those situations often turn to God in prayer. Prayer eases stress; but many people pray more in high-stress situations than they normally do.

The Effect of Prayer on Well-Being Issues

Have you prayed to God in the last seven days?

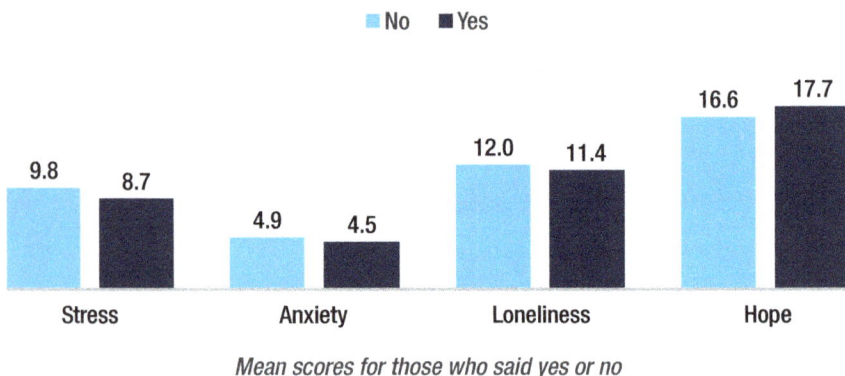

■ No   ■ Yes

	Stress	Anxiety	Loneliness	Hope
No	9.8	4.9	12.0	16.6
Yes	8.7	4.5	11.4	17.7

Mean scores for those who said yes or no

WELL-BEING AND FAITH

We read in Philippians 4:6, "Do not be anxious about anything, but in every situation, by prayer and petition, with thanksgiving, present your requests to God" (NIV). In this and multiple other passages, the Bible urges us to avoid anxiety.

You might be sighing, "Oh, if it were only that easy!" To be sure, there's a learning curve. The Bible shows us an impressive collection of people through the centuries who learned to trust God. But it wasn't easy. Moses struck a rock, Elijah ran to a desert cave, Peter sank into the sea. And yet it's clear that those who move through this learning process—in a dynamic relationship with God—find resources to deal with the stress and anxiety of life.

On that basis, we theorize that regular interaction with God—not only in prayer but in meaningful Bible interaction and worship—should result in less stress and anxiety. We also believe that God's regular reminders that *he is with us* may ease feelings of loneliness and *the biblical vision of a glorious future* may bolster hope.

While the Self-Care section of our survey focused on five specific actions, asking if people had done them the previous seven days, we also have a lot of data on Bible reading. Could we compare, say, the stress levels of those who report using the Bible at least weekly with those doing Self-Care activities within the past week? The results are strong.

Weekly Bible Use and Well-Being Issues

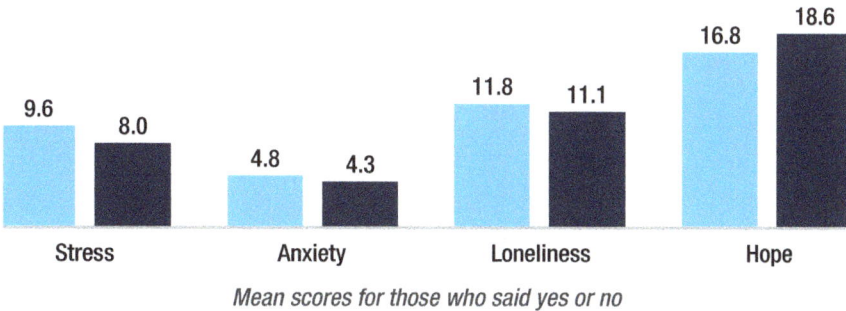

Use the Bible on own weekly or more

No   Yes

Mean scores for those who said yes or no

How does church involvement figure into this equation? For this, we employ our Faith Participation breakdown.

Faith Participation and Well-Being Issues

Non-Christian   Nominal   Casual   Practicing Christian

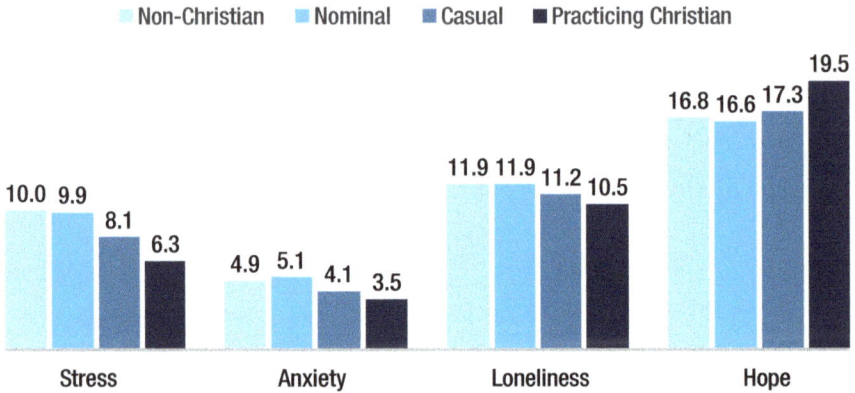

	Stress	Anxiety	Loneliness	Hope
Non-Christian	10.0	4.9	11.9	16.8
Nominal	9.9	5.1	11.9	16.6
Casual	8.1	4.1	11.2	17.3
Practicing Christian	6.3	3.5	10.5	19.5

Nominal Christians (who say they're Christians but rarely attend church) have nearly the same levels as Non-Christians. They report slightly *more* anxiety and *less* hope.

Casual Christians show significantly better numbers across the board, and Practicing Christians (who attend church and also consider their faith very important) display even better scores in every category. In fact, these are better numbers than any of the Self-Care activities have.

So, if you want to ward off stress, anxiety, or loneliness, or if you want to nourish your sense of hope, you could go out for a jog or chat with a friend. Those Self-Care activities are indeed associated with better scores in all those areas. But according to these numbers, it would be even *more* beneficial to gather regularly with a church that reminds you how important your faith is. And this has eternal benefits as well.

COMFORT AND CARE

Did you know that the word comfort, in one form or another, appears nine times in the first seven verses of 2 Corinthians? The Bible is full of comfort—not always at that frequency, but it's a regular feature. In various places, Scripture affirms that we will face problems, but we will also be helped and consoled by a loving Lord. Stress, anxiety, and loneliness are but a few of the things that drag us down, but he will lift us up.

This is one of the repeated patterns of Scripture. Challenge, opposition, sometimes failure, sometimes sin, leading to humbling, repentance, comfort, and restoration. Those who grab a few verses here and there might miss this. But those who *engage*—learning, questioning, applying God's truth to their own circumstances—know this story by heart.

So once again we offer a theory: In difficult times, those who are Scripture Engaged will embrace a God of comfort in ways that others don't. Once again, our expectations are confirmed.

> In difficult times, those who are Scripture Engaged will embrace a God of comfort in ways that others don't.

It's great to see that nearly three-quarters of the Movable Middle (73%) find comfort in their faith in God, at least "somewhat." But the Scripture Engaged seem *sure* of this, nearly everyone agreeing and five of six "strongly."

The Comfort of Faith, by Scripture Engagement

*"I consider my faith to be a great source of comfort
when I am struggling with life issues."*

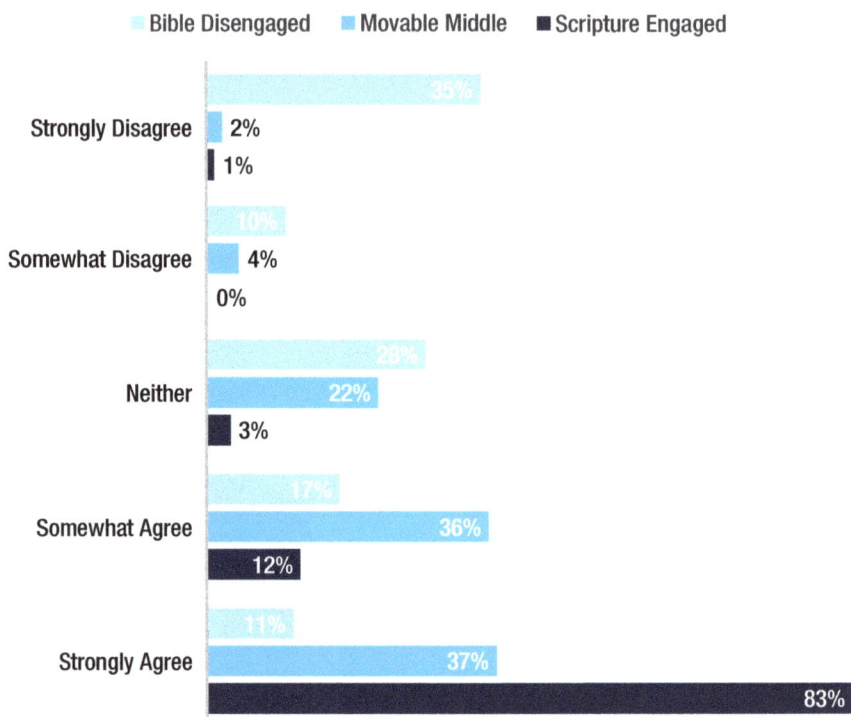

■ Bible Disengaged   ■ Movable Middle   ■ Scripture Engaged

Strongly Disagree
- 35%
- 2%
- 1%

Somewhat Disagree
- 10%
- 4%
- 0%

Neither
- 28%
- 22%
- 3%

Somewhat Agree
- 17%
- 36%
- 12%

Strongly Agree
- 11%
- 37%
- 83%

We see the importance of regular Bible interaction even more vividly as we put together the responses to two different survey questions regarding frequency of Bible use and awareness of God's comfort.

The progression is clear: The more people turn to Scripture, the greater their awareness of God's care for them. They will get stressed. They will face loneliness and anxiety. They will suffer trauma and loss and confusion and sickness. But they also know that the Lord's mercies are new every morning. They can cast their cares upon him, because he cares deeply for them.

Awareness that God Cares, by Frequency of Bible Use

When you use the Bible, how often do you experience . . .
Awareness that God cares deeply about your suffering?

—●— Most of the Time/Always   —●— Rarely/Never

	Three or four times a year	Once a month	Once a week	Several times a week	Four or more times a week	Every day
Most of the Time/Always	52%	53%	66%	83%	91%	94%
Rarely/Never	22%	11%	10%	5%	2%	0%

BODY AND SOUL

"Take care of yourself." Not a bad idea, and as we've seen, there are proven benefits to such Self-Care activities as exercising, seeing friends, and praying. God made us, body and soul, and caring for one part strengthens our whole self. But the Bible reminds us that our greatest strength comes from a trusting relationship with God— "Love the Lord your God with all your heart, with all your soul, and with all your mind" (Matthew 22:37; Deuteronomy 6:5).

Any of the five Self-Care activities might enhance that relationship, but God cares where we place our focus. Is the goal to take care of ourselves, or to open ourselves to God?

It makes sense to invest in our own health, relationships, and peace of mind, but there is a longer-term horizon to keep in view. In the New Testament we read, "Physical exercise has some value, but spiritual exercise is valuable in every way, because it promises life both for the present and for the future" (1 Timothy 4:8).

Weekly Self-Care and Well-Being Issues

Scores of those who have done this within the previous week

	Stress (lower is better)	Anxiety (lower is better)	Loneliness (lower is better)	Hope (higher is better)
Physical Exercise	8.0	4.2	11.2	18.0
Spend Time with a Friend	8.3	4.3	11.1	18.0
Volunteer in my Community	7.4	3.9	10.7	19.0
Meditate	8.9	4.7	11.3	18.3
Pray to God	8.7	4.5	11.4	17.7
Read the Bible	8.0	4.3	11.1	18.6

Through the centuries, believers have conducted such "spiritual exercise" in many ways, some of which resemble our Self-Care activities. These are sometimes called "soul care." Meditation, for example, has long been part of caring for the soul—not to empty the mind, but to focus it on God. Similarly with prayer, it's not just a crying out in times of need (though that's important too), but a communion *with* God, listening as well as speaking. Soul care might also include service, community, fasting, and Sabbath-keeping. And of course the key soul care element is the reading (and contemplation and living out) of Scripture, both in a community of believers and personally.

We've already seen how weekly Bible interaction is associated with lower stress and anxiety, less loneliness, and greater hope. As a Self-Care activity, Bible Reading compares well with the five we've already presented, but, as we've noted, its value goes far beyond that. As the anchoring element of soul care, the Bible opens us up to a transformative interaction—a relationship—with God. ▪

WELL-BEING AND SOUL CARE

Alongside this chapter, we interviewed two guests on the *State of the Bible Podcast*.

Dr. Christine Arnzen is a licensed professional counselor and professor of counseling at Concordia University's Townsend Institute and speaks on self-care and well-being.

Mindy Caliguire is co-founder and president of Soul Care, an organization that supports pastors and leaders in their demanding ministry callings.

Self-Care and Well-Being

Self-Care Activities, U.S. Adults

Percent of those doing these activities in the last seven days

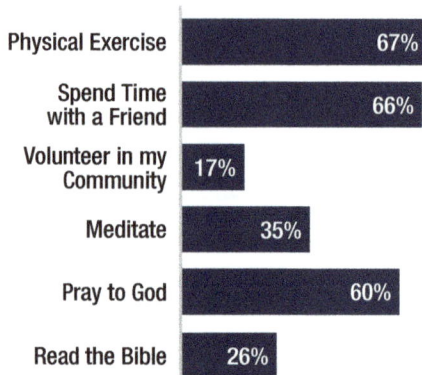

Activity	Percent
Physical Exercise	67%
Spend Time with a Friend	66%
Volunteer in my Community	17%
Meditate	35%
Pray to God	60%
Read the Bible	26%

Self-Care and Human Flourishing

Human Flourishing scores of those doing (or not doing) these activities in the last seven days

■ Yes ■ No

Activity	Yes	No
Physical Exercise	7.4	6.5
Spend Time with a Friend	7.4	6.6
Volunteer in my Community	7.7	7.0
Meditate	7.4	6.9
Pray to God	7.3	6.7
Read the Bible	7.6	6.9

Faith as Comfort

I consider my faith to be a great source of comfort when I am struggling with life issues . . . strongly agree

11%	37%	83%
Bible Disengaged	Movable Middle	Scripture Engaged

Awareness that God Cares, by Frequency of Bible Use

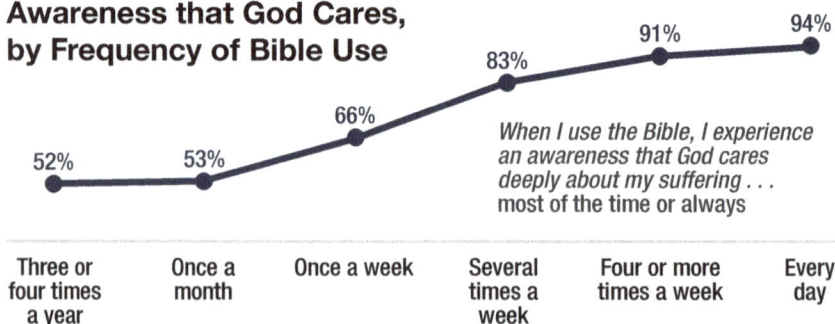

When I use the Bible, I experience an awareness that God cares deeply about my suffering . . . most of the time or always

Three or four times a year	Once a month	Once a week	Several times a week	Four or more times a week	Every day
52%	53%	66%	83%	91%	94%

CHAPTER 5

CHURCH ENGAGEMENT

t looks like a target: concentric circles with "Core" in the bull's eye, progressing outward through Committed, Congregation, Crowd, and Community. If you're a church leader, you've probably seen it—and perhaps even used it in a strategy session. While many have created versions of this diagram, it's generally credited to Rick Warren in *The Purpose-Driven Church* (1995).

What does this diagram show us?

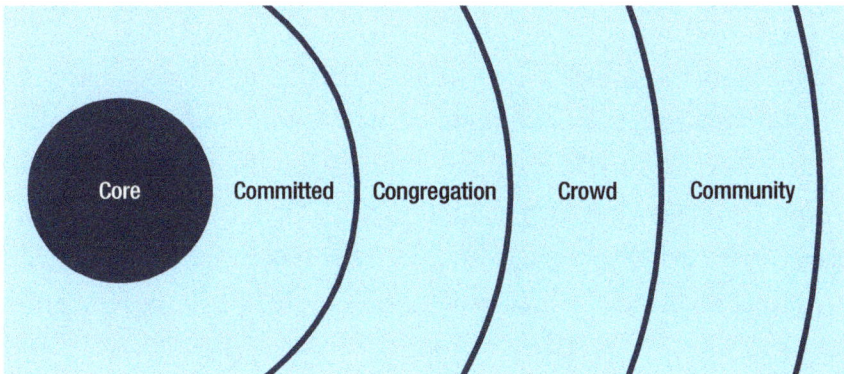

Every church has multiple groups of people connected with it. These groups may have different opinions of God, the Bible, and the church. They may live in different ways, with different habits, struggles, and priorities. Most pertinent to this chapter is the fact that these groups engage with the church at different levels.

Every church leader makes choices about which group or groups to "target." Warren was in the vanguard of those who focused on the outer circles. Many leaders work at drawing a lackadaisical congregation into greater commitment. Others try to strengthen the core.

We focus on the Bible, not church-growth strategy. Yet we routinely see strong statistical connections between engagement with Scripture and engagement with church. People learn *from their church* how to read, understand, and live out the Bible. So we've gathered some insights on how people connect with their local church—in any of the circles—in the hope that we might find fresh ways to draw them into a Bible-driven relationship with God. We also recognize that Scripture consistently calls us into a deeper relationship with God, *and with the people of God.*

FINDING A NEW MEASURE

Some business consulting models evaluate "employee engagement." Do workers believe in the value of their work—and therefore give it their best effort? Do they feel respected in their teams? Do they respect the company and share its goals? Various surveys identify aspects of workplace engagement, and experts are quick to point out ways a company can enhance its productivity by becoming a better place to work.

Are there similar dynamics at church? We believe there are, and that we can measure certain aspects of it. We define **Church Engagement** as "the level of an individual's involvement in the life, mission, and community of a local church. It includes learning and growing in one's faith, meaningful relationships with people in the church, and active use of one's gifts in the work of the church."

Studying aspects of workplace engagement, we found quite a few that transferred neatly to church life, with some adaptation and development. This gives us five new items for our 2025 survey.

Aspects of Church Engagement

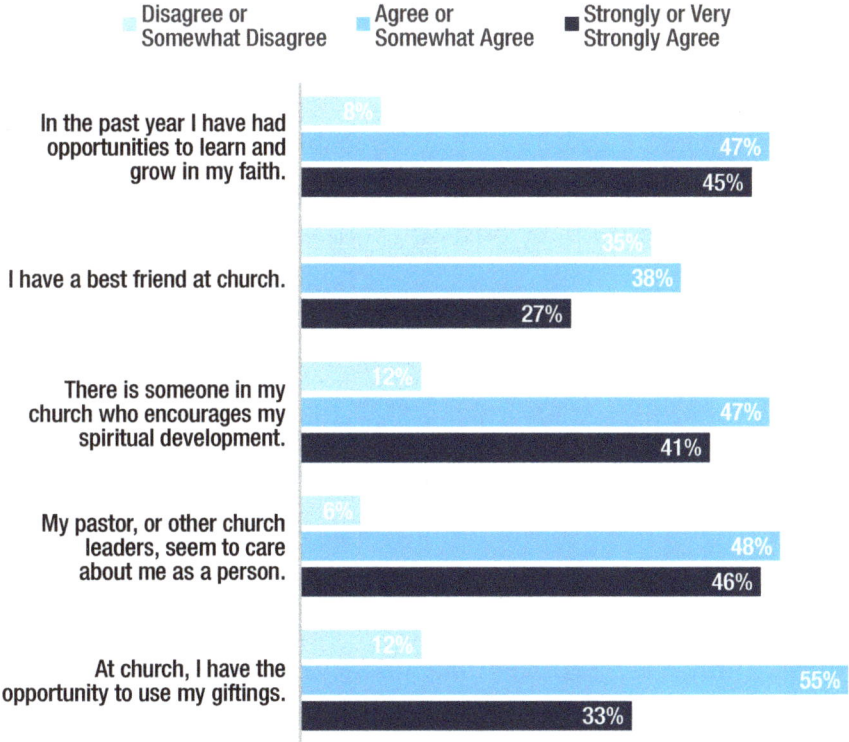

Disagree or Somewhat Disagree | Agree or Somewhat Agree | Strongly or Very Strongly Agree

	Disagree or Somewhat Disagree	Agree or Somewhat Agree	Strongly or Very Strongly Agree
In the past year I have had opportunities to learn and grow in my faith.	8%	47%	45%
I have a best friend at church.	35%	38%	27%
There is someone in my church who encourages my spiritual development.	12%	47%	41%
My pastor, or other church leaders, seem to care about me as a person.	6%	48%	46%
At church, I have the opportunity to use my giftings.	12%	55%	33%

Base: Christians who have attended church in the past six months

Nearly half of Christian church attenders (46%) feel "strongly" that their pastor, or another church leader, cares for them as a person, and even more (48%) agree with that sentiment, though not as strongly. Only one in twenty (6%) say that's not true. That's a huge affirmation for church leaders.

The numbers are similar when it comes to growth opportunities, with nine of ten (92%) agreeing (to some degree) that church gives them a way "to learn and grow in my faith." Only one in twelve (8%) disagree.

Results are nearly as high with the statement "There is someone in my church who encourages my spiritual development," with only about one in eight (12%) disagreeing.

If there's room for growth here, it's probably in the "opportunity to use my giftings."[1] The number agreeing strongly or very strongly (33%) is much lower than most other questions.

If someone has a "best friend" at church, that would likely support greater engagement, but it doesn't seem terribly alarming that more than a third don't. They might merely have such friends in other spheres of their life.

Please note: While many of the questions in our survey go to a full group that represents all of America, these Church Engagement questions were offered only to 35 percent of that group. Only those who identified as Christians *and* said they had attended a Christian

---

1 "Giftings" might seem like an overly religious term, but we actually borrowed it from a secular study of workplace engagement.

church within the last six months received this section. Keep this in mind as we report on subgroups in the rest of this chapter—the Church Engagement questions only went to churchgoing Christians.

Christian Identity and Church Attendance

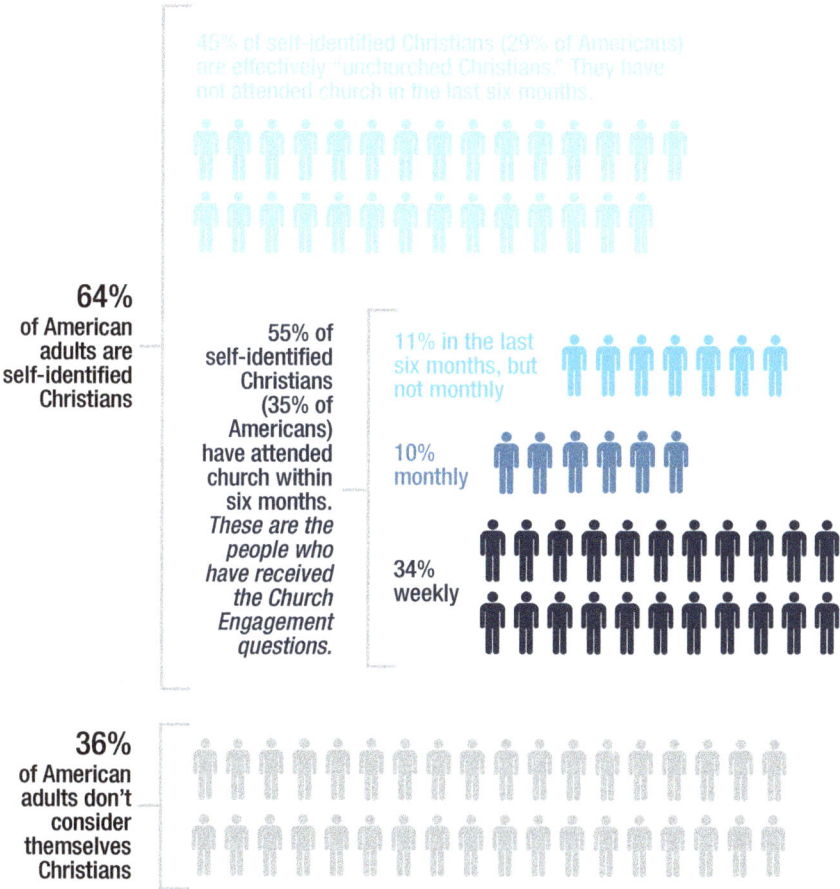

45% of self-identified Christians (29% of Americans) are effectively "unchurched Christians." They have not attended church in the last six months.

64%
of American adults are self-identified Christians

55% of self-identified Christians (35% of Americans) have attended church within six months. *These are the people who have received the Church Engagement questions.*

11% in the last six months, but not monthly

10% monthly

34% weekly

36%
of American adults don't consider themselves Christians

The five Church Engagement questions focus on various interactions in the church, but they don't include *frequency of church attendance*. Do we see differences between those who attend twice a year (the minimum for being asked the Church Engagement questions) and others attending weekly, or even monthly? Yes. There is a tight correlation between engagement and attendance.

Church Engagement Aspects by Attendance

Percent who Strongly or Very Strongly Agree

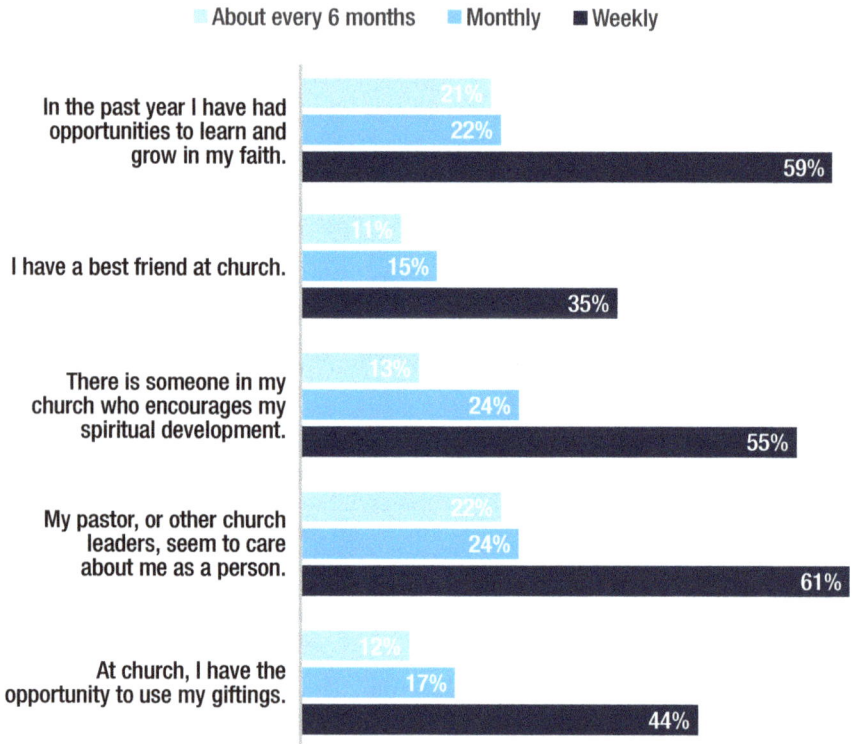

About every 6 months ■ Monthly ■ Weekly

In the past year I have had opportunities to learn and grow in my faith.
- About every 6 months: 21%
- Monthly: 22%
- Weekly: 59%

I have a best friend at church.
- About every 6 months: 11%
- Monthly: 15%
- Weekly: 35%

There is someone in my church who encourages my spiritual development.
- About every 6 months: 13%
- Monthly: 24%
- Weekly: 55%

My pastor, or other church leaders, seem to care about me as a person.
- About every 6 months: 22%
- Monthly: 24%
- Weekly: 61%

At church, I have the opportunity to use my giftings.
- About every 6 months: 12%
- Monthly: 17%
- Weekly: 44%

We expect those who attend weekly to be the most engaged at church, but the striking detail here is the relatively small difference between monthly attenders and those who attend maybe twice a year. Some churches consider people "regular" attenders if they show up once a month, but here we see data to dispute that. Whether we're talking about pastoral care, the use of gifts, or growth opportunities, weekly attenders are more than twice as likely to respond enthusiastically.

CHURCH ENGAGEMENT DEMOGRAPHICS

Generation Z scores lowest in Church Engagement. On every point, they are less likely to agree strongly or very strongly than any other generation. Surprisingly, **Millennials** outscore **Gen X** on several of these questions.

Church Engagement Scores by Generation

Percent who Strongly or Very Strongly Agree

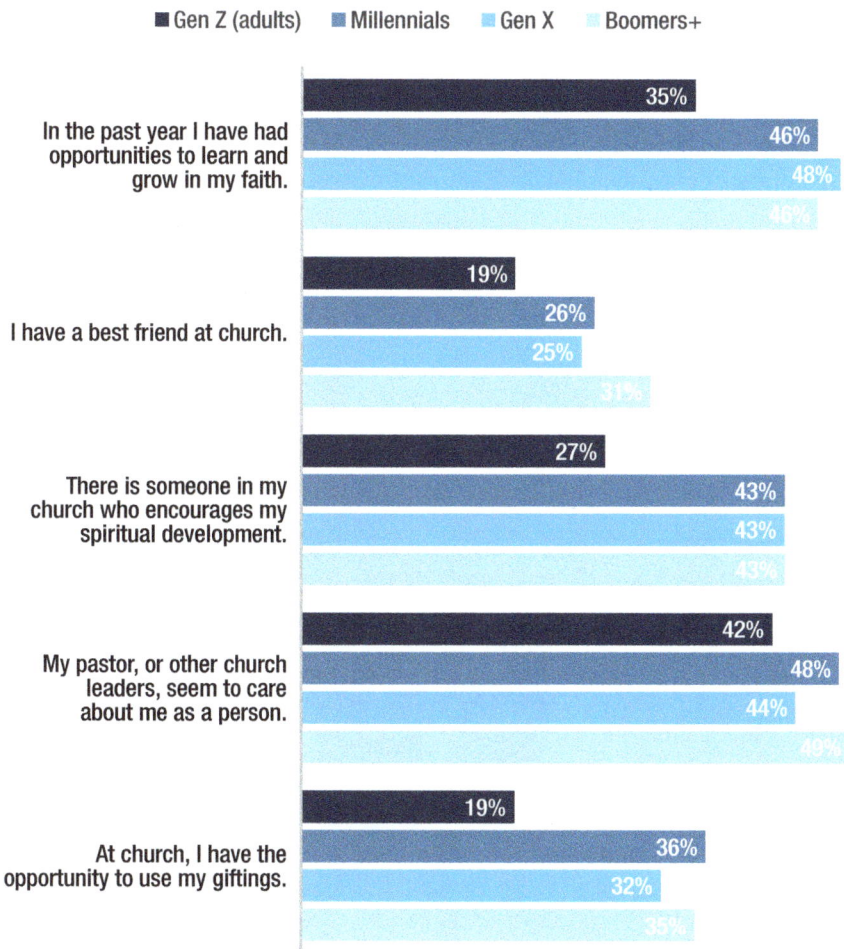

■ Gen Z (adults)   ■ Millennials   ■ Gen X   ■ Boomers+

In the past year I have had opportunities to learn and grow in my faith.
- 35%
- 46%
- 48%
- 46%

I have a best friend at church.
- 19%
- 26%
- 25%
- 31%

There is someone in my church who encourages my spiritual development.
- 27%
- 43%
- 43%
- 43%

My pastor, or other church leaders, seem to care about me as a person.
- 42%
- 48%
- 44%
- 49%

At church, I have the opportunity to use my giftings.
- 19%
- 36%
- 32%
- 35%

The greatest disparity for Gen Z appears with "I have the opportunity to use my giftings." It may be that these young people don't yet know their spiritual gifts or how to use them (along with their physical and intellectual gifts) in the church. But we also know that some churches make it difficult to break into meaningful ministry roles. The older edge of Generation Z turns 28 this year; perhaps we could do more to help them recognize and use their God-given abilities.

When we separate high, average, and low Church Engagement scores,[2] we get an interesting perspective on gender differences. While men were more likely to demonstrate *average* church engagement (50% to 43%), women were better represented at the *high* and *low* ends of this spectrum. This difference comes entirely from the giftings question. We recognize that churches differ in theology and practice related to the gifts women may use, and this might contribute to these responses.

Levels of Church Engagement by Gender

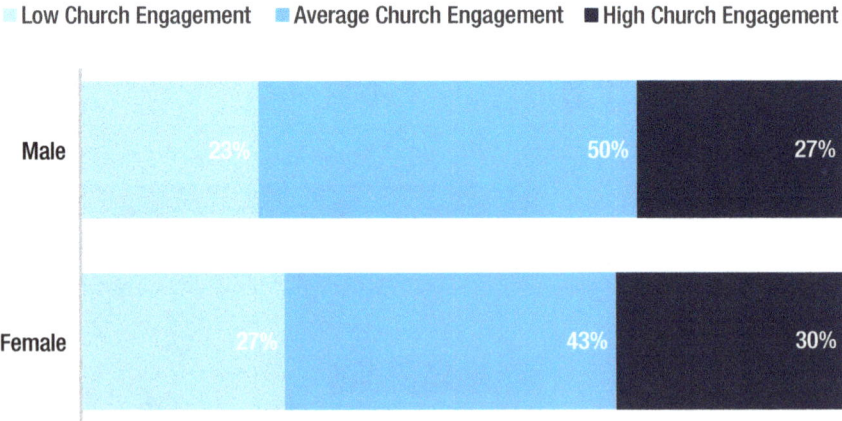

■ Low Church Engagement　　■ Average Church Engagement　　■ High Church Engagement

	Low	Average	High
Male	23%	50%	27%
Female	27%	43%	30%

2 Responses get a point value of 1 (Disagree) to 6 (Very Strongly Agree). The five questions are totaled for a range of 5–30. We designate full scores of 24–30 "high," 17–23 "average," and 5–16 "low."

Married people are significantly more likely than **never-married people** to be highly engaged with church (32% to 23%). Some of this may be generational, as many in the low-engaged Generation Z are not married yet, but it shouldn't surprise us that those who have never engaged themselves in a marriage are also shying away from engagement with a church. Divorced people register in between the married and never married.[3]

Levels of Church Engagement by Marital Status

Low Church Engagement   Average Church Engagement   High Church Engagement

Marital Status	Low	Average	High
Married	23%	45%	32%
Never Married	28%	50%	23%
Divorced	25%	49%	25%

Another demographic factor of note is **community size**. The survey asks people where they live.

- Urban (area of 250,000 people or more)
- Suburb (city or town near a large city)
- City (30,000 to 250,000 people)
- Small city (5,000 to 30,000 people)
- Rural (less than 5,000 people)

---

3 Small sample sizes for the Separated and Widowed make those results unreliable.

People living in smaller communities and rural areas have significantly higher Church Engagement. Rural and small-town residents boast Church Engagement at a level half-again higher than those living in suburbs or medium-level cities.

Levels of Church Engagement by Community Size

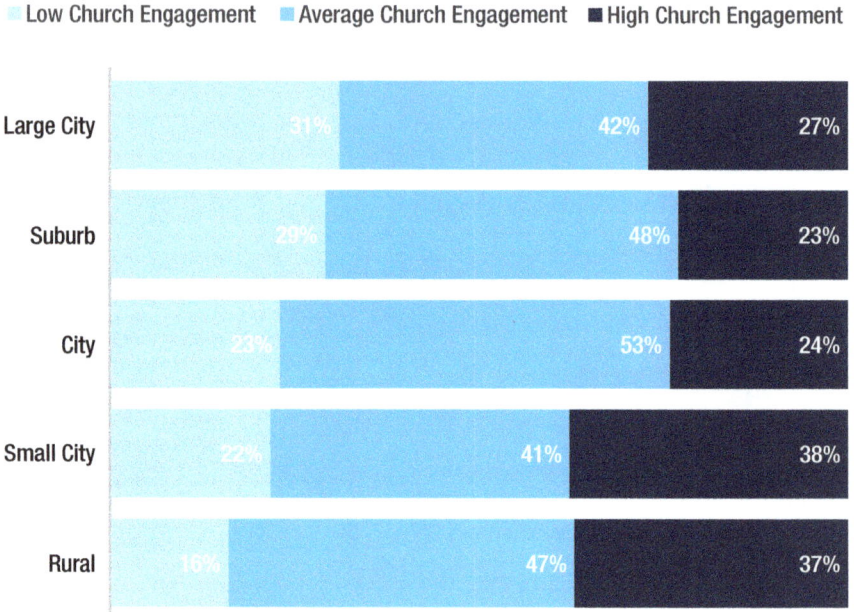

Low Church Engagement ■ Average Church Engagement ■ High Church Engagement

Community	Low	Average	High
Large City	31%	42%	27%
Suburb	29%	48%	23%
City	23%	53%	24%
Small City	22%	41%	38%
Rural	16%	47%	37%

CHURCH ENGAGEMENT, FLOURISHING, AND WELL-BEING

In the last two chapters, we've explored a variety of conditions under the titles of Human Flourishing and Well-Being. Our data show that Scripture Engaged people tend to be highly flourishing as well. And those who read the Bible regularly report lower stress and anxiety, less loneliness, and greater hope.

Now we turn our analysis to Church Engagement. Do Church Engaged people have better lives—as measured by the elements of Human Flourishing and factors of stress, loneliness, and hope?

A strong majority (62%) of people with high Church Engagement are also at the highest level of Human Flourishing. Only one in twelve of them (8%) are at the lowest Human Flourishing level. The strong association continues through the average and low levels of Church Engagement. With less Church Engagement comes less flourishing.

Human Flourishing by Church Engagement

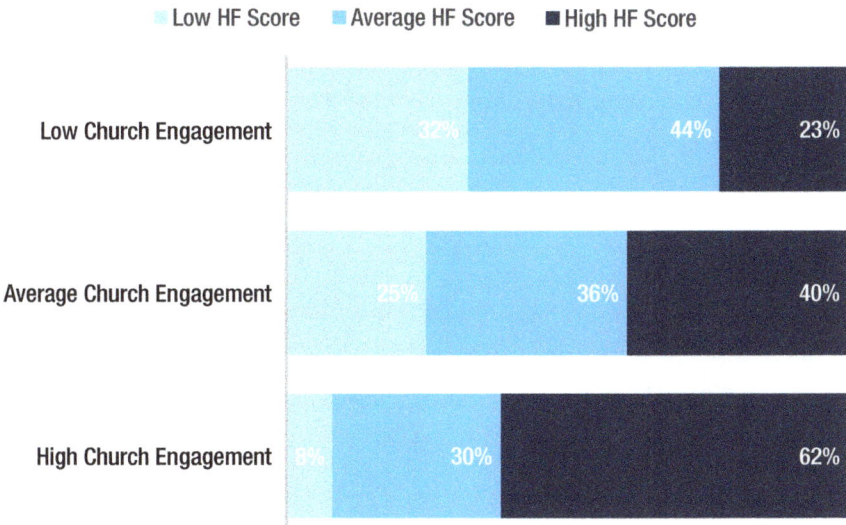

Low HF Score   Average HF Score   High HF Score

Church Engagement	Low HF Score	Average HF Score	High HF Score
Low Church Engagement	32%	44%	23%
Average Church Engagement	25%	36%	40%
High Church Engagement	8%	30%	62%

As you may recall, the Human Flourishing Index includes questions on five different domains of life. People with high Church Engagement score higher on all five of these domains, but the difference is especially great in two of them—Meaning & Purpose and Close Social Relationships.

Selected Flourishing Domains by Church Engagement

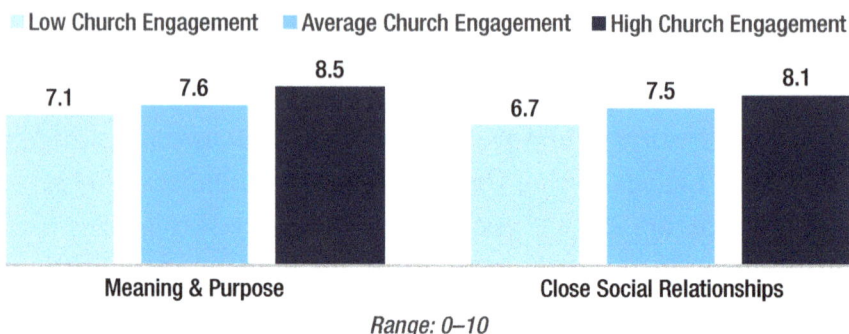

■ Low Church Engagement ■ Average Church Engagement ■ High Church Engagement

Meaning & Purpose			Close Social Relationships		
7.1	7.6	8.5	6.7	7.5	8.1

Range: 0–10

This makes sense. While church involvement might help with Mental & Physical Health, Life Satisfaction, and Character & Virtue (and we do see some increase in these domains for the Church Engaged), it clearly provides opportunities in matters of purpose and relationship.[4]

WELL-BEING

If you are involved enough at church to direct the children's Christmas program, you might argue that church engagement leads to *more* stress and anxiety. Yet our survey finds that, in general, high Church Engagement is associated with lower stress and anxiety, as well as less loneliness and greater hope. The connection is not as strong as we see with Scripture Engagement, but it's substantial—a drop of about 40 percent in stress scores, 20 percent less loneliness, and nearly a 20 percent jump in the hope score. Church Engagement is good for us.

---

4 The Secure Flourishing Index takes the five Human Flourishing domains and adds one—Financial & Material Stability. Even this domain has a substantial increase among the High Church Engaged, though the jump is not as great as we see in the Purpose or Relationship domains.

Selected Well-Being Factors by Church Engagement

■ Low Church Engagement   ■ Average Church Engagement   ■ High Church Engagement

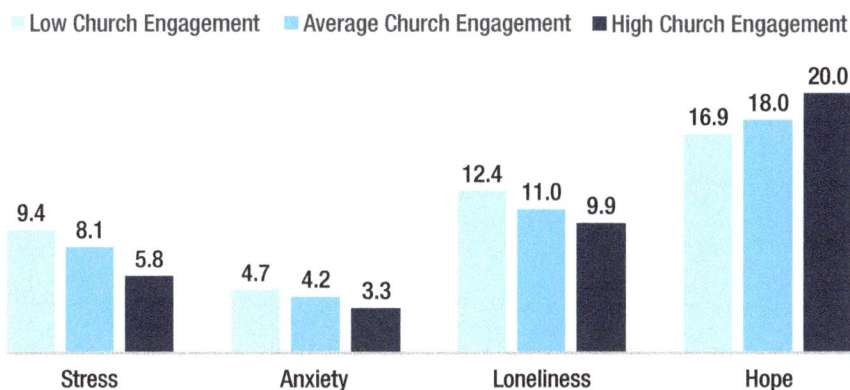

	Stress	Anxiety	Loneliness	Hope
Low Church Engagement	9.4	4.7	12.4	16.9
Average Church Engagement	8.1	4.2	11.0	18.0
High Church Engagement	5.8	3.3	9.9	20.0

Ranges: Stress 0–40, Anxiety 0–20, Loneliness 5–20, Hope 3–24

CHURCH, FAITH, AND BIBLE

Church Engagement is not the same as Scripture Engagement, though they overlap. Scripture Engagement is about frequency of Bible interaction but also the Bible's centrality in our decision-making and its impact on our relationships with God and others. Our newly created category of Church Engagement gathers several aspects of church relationships, service, and spiritual development. It's a different measure, but we would still expect many Scripture Engaged people to be Church Engaged as well. And vice versa.

Statistically, that's what we find—considerable overlap, but not absolute unity. In the three Scripture Engagement groups, we find just over half of each group also in the corresponding Church Engagement group. A majority (56%) of the Movable Middle are in the Average Church Engagement group, and the Bible Disengaged have a similar overlap (52%) with Low Church Engagement. Yet two out of five Scripture Engaged people (40%) are only at a level of Average Church Engagement. They have a strong relationship with the Bible, but apparently not as strong a relationship with their church.

Church Engagement by Scripture Engagement

■ Low Church Engagement   ■ Average Church Engagement   ■ High Church Engagement

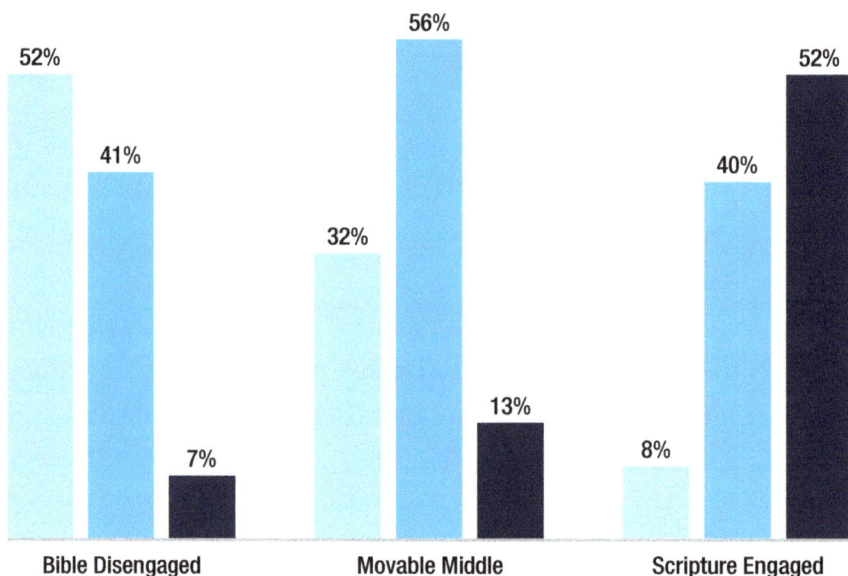

Bible Disengaged
- 52%
- 41%
- 7%

Movable Middle
- 32%
- 56%
- 13%

Scripture Engaged
- 8%
- 40%
- 52%

DENOMINATIONS

Do certain kinds of churches foster greater Church Engagement? Yes, among four major denominational groups, we see significant differences in the percentage of those with high Church Engagement: Evangelical Protestant (39%); Mainline Protestant (30%); Historically Black Protestant (19%); and Roman Catholic (12%).[5] We

5 The sample size for Orthodox Christian was too small to yield reliable results.

recognize that our selection of the Church Engagement items may reflect an evangelical bias, and that other groups may have different beliefs about what a church should be or do, so we're careful in evaluating these numbers.

The item that gave the greatest edge to Evangelicals was "There is someone in my church who encourages my spiritual development," with more than half (54%) agreeing strongly or very strongly (Mainline had 38%; Historically Black 29%; Catholic 24%).

Church Engagement Level by Denomination Group

■ Low Church Engagement   ■ Average Church Engagement   ■ High Church Engagement

	Low	Average	High
Evangelical	18%	43%	39%
Mainline Protestant	27%	43%	30%
Historically Black Denominations	19%	62%	19%
Catholic	37%	51%	12%

HOW PEOPLE ATTEND

Most church attenders (72%) do so primarily in person. About one-eighth (12%) attend primarily online, and about one-sixth (16%) say they attend both ways "about equally." So, which group has the greatest Church Engagement?

In-person attenders have the highest percentage of highly Church Engaged (31%), compared to only 19 percent of those who attend primarily online and 23 percent of those who attend both ways. One contributing factor may be that in-person attenders do so more frequently. Nearly two-thirds of them (66%) come to church weekly, compared to just 46 percent of those who tune in online.

When we examine "strong" and "very strong" agreement on each of the five items of church engagement, we see those who physically come to services outpacing the others on every point. The smallest difference, oddly, is for "I have a best friend at church" (28% in person; 23% online; 25% both). The widest spread occurs with "My pastor, or other church leaders, seem to care about me as a person" (51% in person; 33% online; 36% both).

Church Engagement Level by How People Attend

Percent agreeing strongly or very strongly with each statement

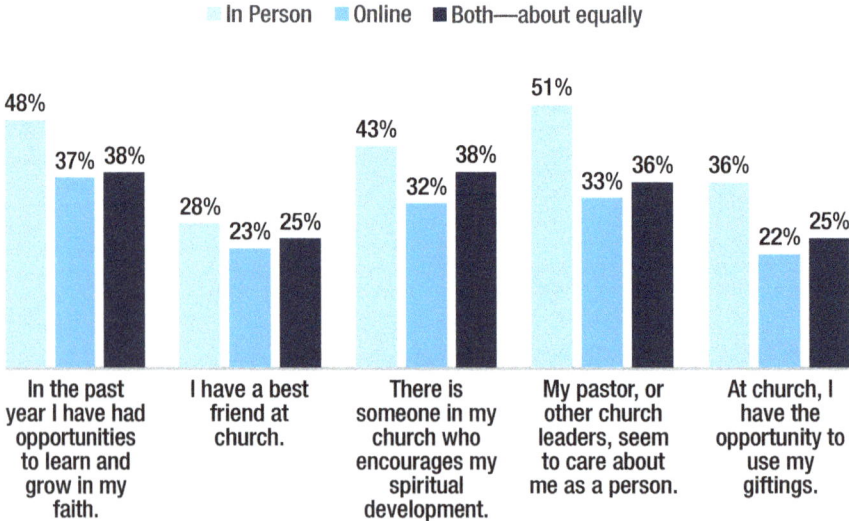

■ In Person ■ Online ■ Both—about equally

	In Person	Online	Both—about equally
In the past year I have had opportunities to learn and grow in my faith.	48%	37%	38%
I have a best friend at church.	28%	23%	25%
There is someone in my church who encourages my spiritual development.	43%	32%	38%
My pastor, or other church leaders, seem to care about me as a person.	51%	33%	36%
At church, I have the opportunity to use my giftings.	36%	22%	25%

CHURCH ENGAGEMENT AND RELEVANCE

This year, in our participation in the worldwide Patmos Survey (see chapter 2), we introduced a few new items in our poll.

- "Church leaders often make the Bible relevant to my life."
- "Church leaders encourage me to read the Bible."

These are not part of our Church Engagement metric, but they provide validation for it. With both statements, 90 percent of those at the highest level of Church Engagement agree strongly or very strongly. That's more than twice the percentage seen from those at the "average" level.

Relevance and Encouragement
by Level of Church Engagement

Percent agreeing strongly or very strongly with each statement

■ Low Church Engagement   ■ Average Church Engagement   ■ High Church Engagement

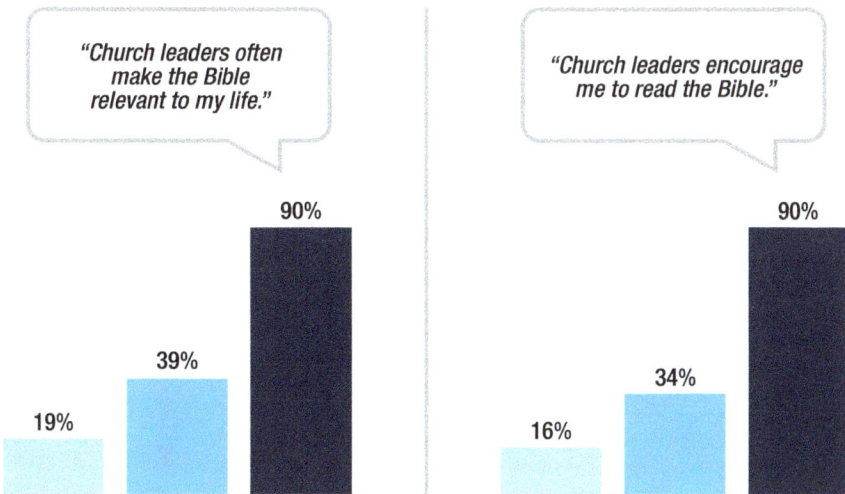

"Church leaders often make the Bible relevant to my life."

19%   39%   90%

"Church leaders encourage me to read the Bible."

16%   34%   90%

If you're a church leader seeking to improve Church Engagement in your congregation, you could try any number of things. Encourage people's spiritual development and give them opportunities to learn and grow and use their gifts. But also urge them to read the Bible on their own, even as you keep showing how important the Bible can be in the details of their lives.

The Bible is more than a book, and church-going is more than an appointment. Both of them build our relationship with God and others. Both change our lives. And, as we've seen throughout this chapter, the two are statistically connected. Scripture Engagement and Church Engagement operate in tandem.

Transformation by Level of Church Engagement

"The message of the Bible has transformed my life."

Disagree ■ Agree Somewhat ■ Agree Strongly

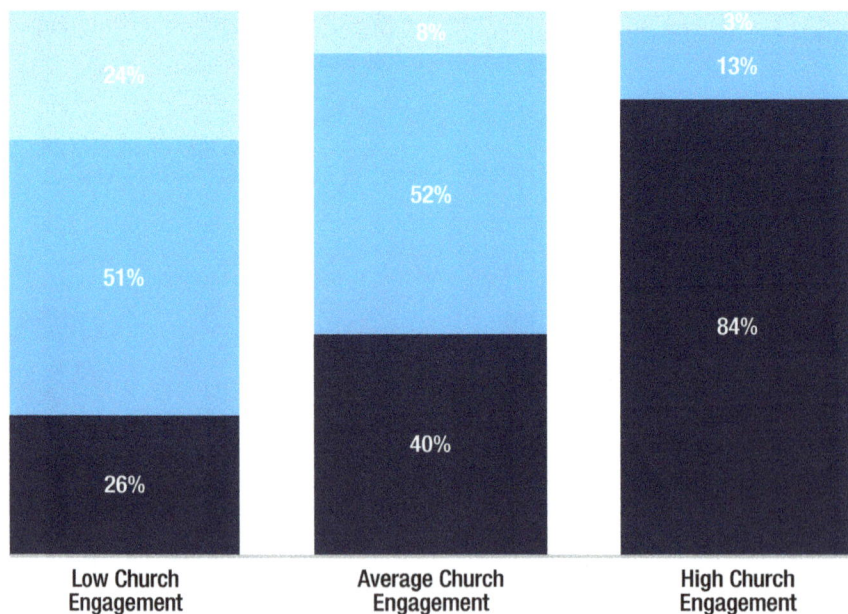

	Disagree	Agree Somewhat	Agree Strongly
Low Church Engagement	24%	51%	26%
Average Church Engagement	8%	52%	40%
High Church Engagement	3%	13%	84%

In closing, we offer one more overlap between these two powerful forces: Bible and church. One question in our survey asks whether people can agree that "The message of the Bible has transformed my life." We wanted to see how people at different levels of church engagement responded. These are all self-identified Christians, and yet when people are ho-hum about church, they also seem to be unsure about biblical transformation. But those who engage with the church, growing in faith and knowledge, using their gifts and making friends—the vast majority of these people agree "strongly" that the Word of God has changed them. ■

WHAT DOES CHURCH ENGAGEMENT LOOK LIKE?

Peter Englert is the Adult Ministries Director at Browncroft Community Church in Rochester, New York. He shares how his church is working to encourage the spiritual growth of individuals and foster a healthy and supportive church community in their city.

State of the Bible
THE PODCAST

AMERICAN BIBLE SOCIETY

Church Engagement

Church Commitment

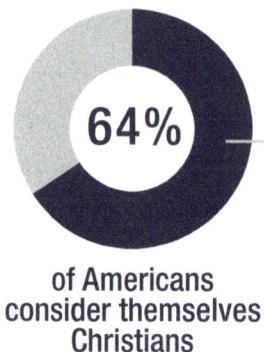

64%

of Americans consider themselves Christians

45%
of Christians don't attend church

55%
of Christians have attended within the last 6 months*

11%
attend about twice a year

10%
attend monthly

34%
attend weekly

These are the people who received the Church Engagement questions.

Church Engagement Items

Percent who Strongly or Very Strongly Agree

■ All Generations ■ Gen Z

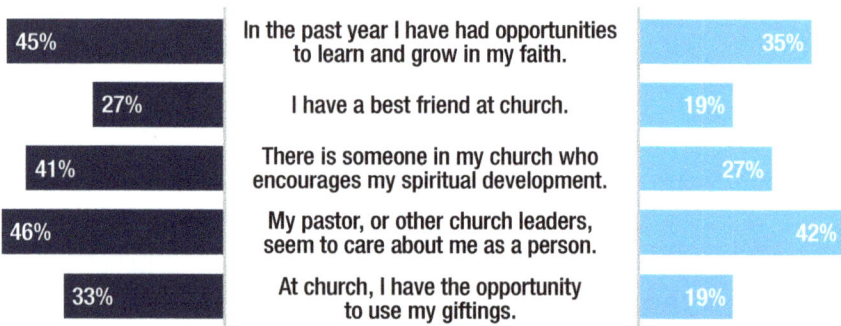

Item	All Generations	Gen Z
In the past year I have had opportunities to learn and grow in my faith.	45%	35%
I have a best friend at church.	27%	19%
There is someone in my church who encourages my spiritual development.	41%	27%
My pastor, or other church leaders, seem to care about me as a person.	46%	42%
At church, I have the opportunity to use my giftings.	33%	19%

The Bible and Church Engagement (CE)

"The message of the Bible has transformed my life."

■ Disagree
■ Agree Somewhat
■ Agree Strongly

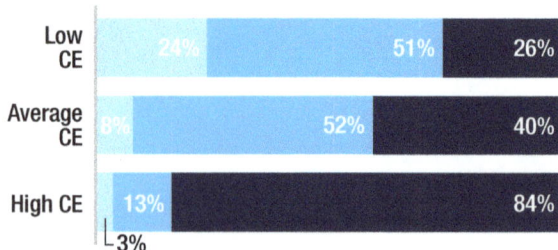

	Disagree	Agree Somewhat	Agree Strongly
Low CE	24%	51%	26%
Average CE	8%	52%	40%
High CE	3%	13%	84%

CHAPTER 6

IDENTITY

Who are you? Perhaps you've had to describe yourself in a job application or a LinkedIn blurb. Once you get past name, age, home, family, job . . . what do you say then? Some companies make their employees complete personality tests, emerging with detailed profiles. Are you a Thinker or Feeler? Do you exert Openness or Conscientiousness? Are you a driven "3" or an easygoing "9"?

Yet somehow we know our identity can't be defined by a number or a string of letters. We are also shaped by priorities and core beliefs, not to mention family, culture, community, and personal experience. As Christians we find our true selves in Jesus—and yet one believer's sense of identity will be quite different from another's.

So . . . who are you?

All these factors make it a challenge to survey identity on a large scale, yet we've found that people's sense of identity often affects their spiritual development, especially among younger adults (many of whom are separating their identity from that of their parents, choosing to maintain some values while challenging others and embracing new priorities).

So we took up that challenge, setting up a triad of Identity statements and asking people how much they agreed.

- I know who I am.
- I always have a good sense about what is important to me.
- I know what I believe or value.[1]

In a very simple form, these statements address self-image, beliefs, and priorities. The strength of people's responses provides insight into the strength of their sense of identity. We can then compare this with other aspects of demography, well-being, and faith development.[2]

GENERATIONS AND GENDER

According to these numbers, the subgroup with the greatest "identity crisis" is **young men.** (Note that we only survey adults, so these Gen Z males are 18–28 years old. Others have found similar results among younger teens.) Gen Z men have the lowest percentage of

---

1 These statements are derived from the Consolidated sub-scale of the Self-Concept and Identity Measure (SCIM). Kaufman, E. A., Cundiff, J. M., & Crowell, S. E. (2015). The development, factor structure, and validation of the Self-Concept and Identity Measure (SCIM): A self-report assessment of clinical identity disturbance. *Journal of Psychopathology and Behavioral Assessment, 37,* 122–133. https://doi.org/10.1007/s10862-014-9441-2

2 People were asked to indicate the extent to which each statement was "true of me," from 0 to 10. Most responded with 8, 9, or 10, giving an overall mean score of 24.5 for the three statements combined. We have grouped the scores into Weak (0–19), Moderate (19–28), and Strong (28–30) Identity levels.

people who are in the Strong Identity group (30%) and the highest percentage who are in the Weak Identity group (also 30%).

At this age we also see the greatest division between genders with regard to identity. **Gen Z females** show much stronger Identity (41% Strong and only 23% Weak) than males in this group (30% Strong; 30% Weak). Surprisingly, they also boast a stronger sense of identity than their "older sisters" in the Millennial generation (37% Strong and 25% Weak).

Apart from the strong showing of Gen Z females, it seems that a sense of identity **tends to strengthen with age**, as we might expect. Well more than half of the Boomer+ generation, women and men alike, are in the Strong Identity group.

Identity Levels by Generation and Gender

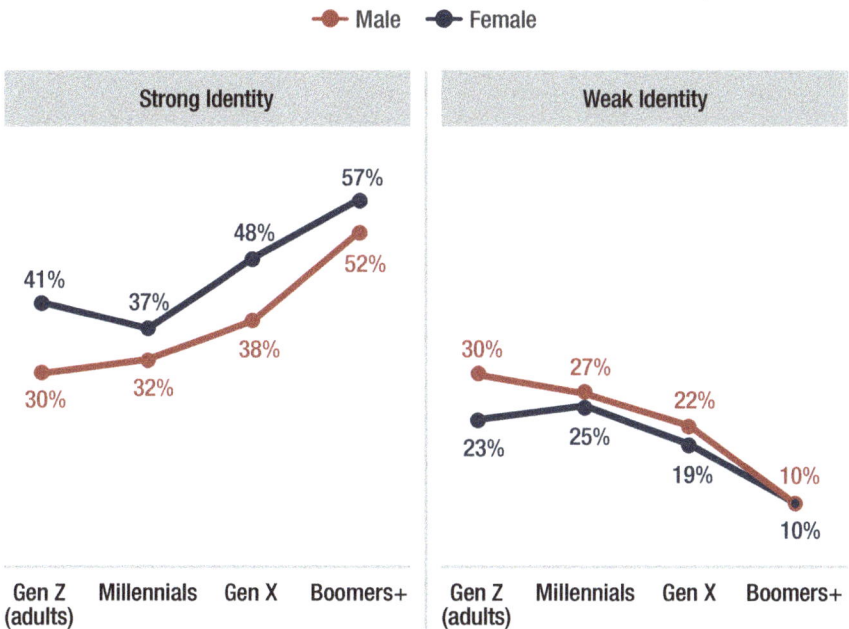

●— Male   ●— Female

Strong Identity	Weak Identity

Strong Identity:
- Female: Gen Z (adults) 41%, Millennials 37%, Gen X 48%, Boomers+ 57%
- Male: Gen Z (adults) 30%, Millennials 32%, Gen X 38%, Boomers+ 52%

Weak Identity:
- Male: Gen Z (adults) 30%, Millennials 27%, Gen X 22%, Boomers+ 10%
- Female: Gen Z (adults) 23%, Millennials 25%, Gen X 19%, Boomers+ 10%

Gen Z (adults)   Millennials   Gen X   Boomers+

As we age,
we learn more
about who
we are, what
we believe,
and what
we consider
important.

It can be argued that young people have permission to be less confident in their identity, since they're still young. As we age, we learn more about who we are, what we believe, and what we consider important. In his foundational work on psychosocial development, James Marcia posited four stages of exploration and commitment. In Stage 2—Identity Foreclosure—someone commits to a certain life-course without much exploration of their own identity. This situation is seen as less healthy than Stage 3—Identity Moratorium—in which someone puts off a decision while they explore the options (think of a "gap year" a student might take before or after college). Our survey may indicate that most older adults are in Stage 4—Identity Achievement—where they've explored who they are and made life commitments accordingly.[3]

Yet others might challenge that assessment, suggesting that our culture discourages parents from teaching children the moral truths that would provide a sturdy foundation on which to build their identity.

MARITAL STATUS

Marriage seems to be an identity builder, or at least an identity *marker*, with nearly half (47%) of married people scoring high. People might

---

3 Marcia, J. E. (1966). Development and validation of ego-identity status. *Journal of Personality and Social Psychology*, 3(5), 551–558. https://doi.org/10.1037/h0023281

strengthen their sense of identity by becoming a spouse, and perhaps a parent. It might also be true that people with a low sense of identity are less willing to commit to a marriage.

In fact, we see that the never-married have a much lower percentage (35%) at the Strong Identity level and many more at the lowest level (28%, compared to 15% for married people). Of course Gen Z is the source of many in the never-married camp, and we've already seen their low Identity scores, but they only move the needle one percentage point. Even without the youngest generation, never-married people have far more with low Identity scores (27%) and far fewer with high scores (36%).

It might surprise some readers that we see the greatest percentage of high Identity scores among divorced people. Divorce is often an identity-shattering process, but these numbers suggest that many people emerge from the pain of divorce (and the required rebuilding) with a greater sense of their individual selves, beliefs, and values.

Identity Levels by Marital Status

■ Weak Identity   ■ Strong Identity

IDENTITY AND WELL-BEING

STRESS

Is it stressful to be unsure of who you are, what you believe, or what's important to you? In a word, yes. Stress scores are much higher for those who have low Identity scores. According to our metrics, those with the strongest sense of identity report 63 percent less stress than those with the weakest identity.

The arrow of causality may sometimes go the other way. Stressful situations may sap a person's sense of identity. If you get fired from your job, for instance, you might experience both an identity crisis and considerable stress. But in many cases, a low sense of self makes the stresses of life worse, and we might be able to ease those stresses with a recommitment to identity—our core purpose and priorities.

Stress Scores by Identity Level

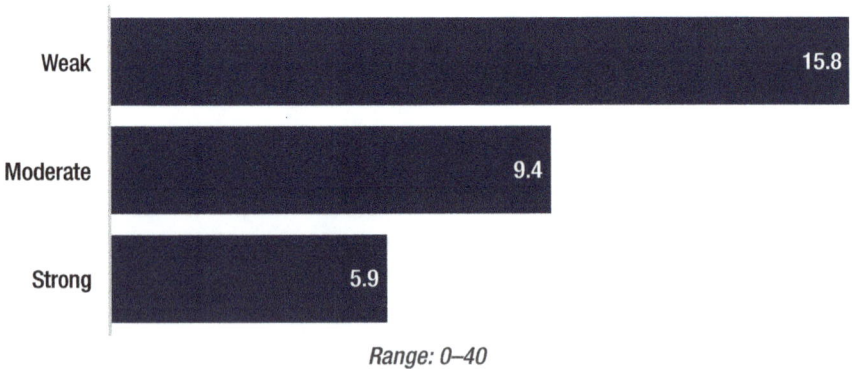

Identity Level	Stress Score
Weak	15.8
Moderate	9.4
Strong	5.9

Range: 0–40

LONELINESS

We sometimes assume that identity is all about the individual. In popular discourse, the Identity statement "I know who I am" is often taken to mean, "I don't care what anyone else says." At least since the Sixties, the rebellious loner has been a pop-culture hero.

But for most of us, our sense of identity is woven into our interactions with others. We might define ourselves as a spouse, parent, friend, or teacher. Our beliefs and values have been crafted in part by family, friends, and church. Even our idea of "what is important" generally has to do with the people around us or how we contribute to the well-being of others.

So it's helpful to compare Identity levels to levels of loneliness, one of the "well-being issues" we examined in our discussion of self-care in Chapter 4 (see page 79). Our findings on both identity and loneliness rely on responses to a set of statements. The Loneliness statements have to do with feeling left out, distant from others, not understood. As we put these two factors together, will we find the "lonely leader," self-confident but isolated? Or will we find that a strong sense of identity pairs well with social connection?

We don't find many "lonely leaders." In fact, there's a clear parallel between a strong sense of identity and *low* loneliness. Only one in nine strong-identity men (11%) and one in five strong-identity women (19%) report high loneliness. Conversely, about half of those with a weak sense of identity (53% of women; 46% of men) report high levels of loneliness.

Identity Levels by Levels of Loneliness

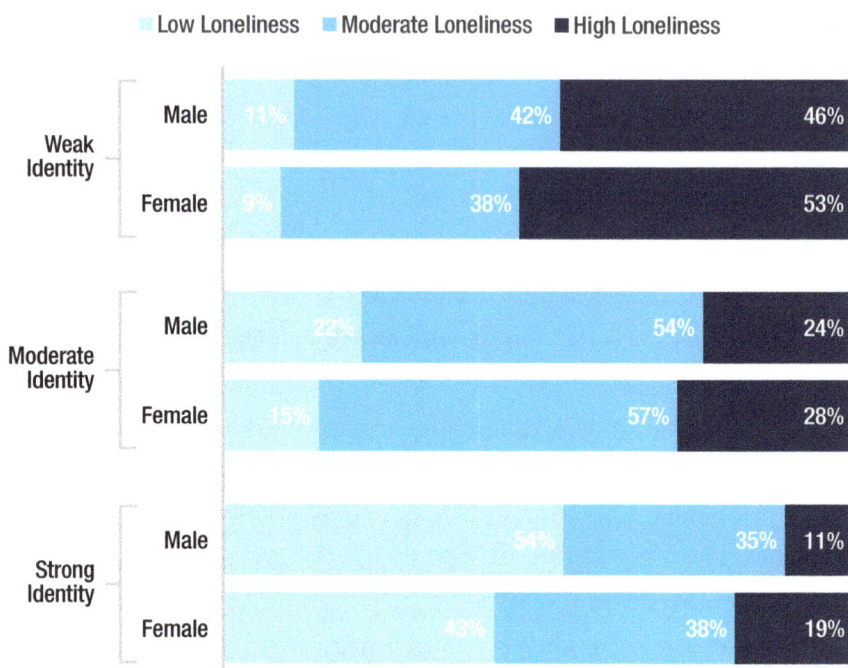

Low Loneliness ■ Moderate Loneliness ■ High Loneliness

Weak Identity

Male: 11% | 42% | 46%
Female: 9% | 38% | 53%

Moderate Identity

Male: 22% | 54% | 24%
Female: 15% | 57% | 28%

Strong Identity

Male: 54% | 35% | 11%
Female: 43% | 38% | 19%

IDENTITY AND SPIRITUAL FACTORS

The Bible has a great deal to say about human identity. We are created in God's image (Genesis 1:27), "a little lower than the angels, … crowned … with glory and honor" (Psalm 8:5 NIV), part of a world God loves (John 3:16). None of this negates the reality that all of us are sinners in need of God's grace (Romans 3:23–24). Yet, in Christ, we are "a new creation" (2 Corinthians 5:17), God's artistic masterpiece (Ephesians 2:10). The Spirit whispers that we are God's children (Romans 8:16).

Scripture says all this, and so we would expect those who engage with Scripture to demonstrate a strong sense of identity. We'd expect the same of people who participate meaningfully in a church, practicing and reinforcing this God-given identity with others. And that's exactly what the numbers show.

Yet we also find another factor. Religious practice in general, whether Christian or not, is associated with strong identity.

Apart from the *content* of any religion's beliefs, scholars have long noted the value of the social identity that comes with *participation* in a religious group. Beyond that, the required rituals or disciplines of any religious group (including Christianity) can give adherents a sense of mastery, enhancing their self-esteem.[4] Note also that our identity score is based partly on a broad question about beliefs and values, elements of virtually every world religion.

Two in five (40%) of those in our survey who follow "Other Religions" (not Christian) agree that "my religious faith is very important to me." This subgroup has 67 percent at the Strong Identity level, suggesting that it's not merely identification with a religion that bolsters identity, but how important they consider it.

That, of course is what we see among Christians as well. Practicing Christians have vastly more representation in the Strong Identity crowd, compared with Casual or Nominal Christians (who have barely more than the Nones).

---

4   Greenfield, E. A., & Marks, N. F. (2007). Religious Social Identity as an Explanatory Factor for Associations between More Frequent Formal Religious Participation and Psychological Well-Being. *The International journal for the psychology of religion, 17(3)*, 245–259. https://doi.org/10.1080/10508610701402309

Identity Levels by Religious Participation

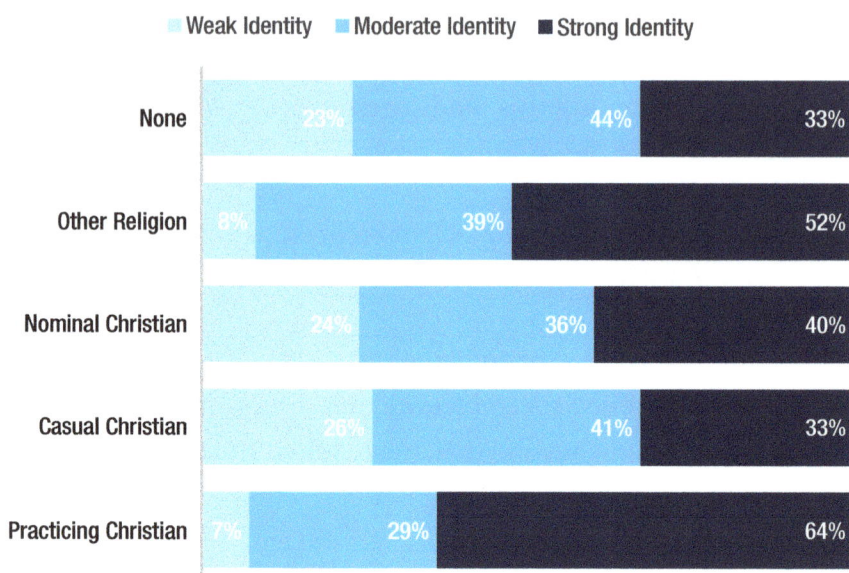

Legend: Weak Identity ▪ Moderate Identity ▪ Strong Identity

Religious Participation	Weak Identity	Moderate Identity	Strong Identity
None	23%	44%	33%
Other Religion	8%	39%	52%
Nominal Christian	24%	36%	40%
Casual Christian	26%	41%	33%
Practicing Christian	7%	29%	64%

SCRIPTURE ENGAGEMENT

As we just saw with Practicing Christians, the Scripture Engaged are far ahead of the pack in strength of identity. Nearly two-thirds of them (63%) are at the highest level. Less than a tenth (9%) are at the weakest level. The sheer discipline of regular Bible reading is likely an identity booster for this group, but remember also that the Scripture Engagement formula includes questions on decision-making. The Scripture Engaged generally indicate that the Bible has a substantial influence on what they buy or watch. Those simple choices can be important identity markers. A person says, "I am a Bible believer, so I will make these everyday decisions with scriptural teaching in mind."

Identity Levels by Scripture Engagement

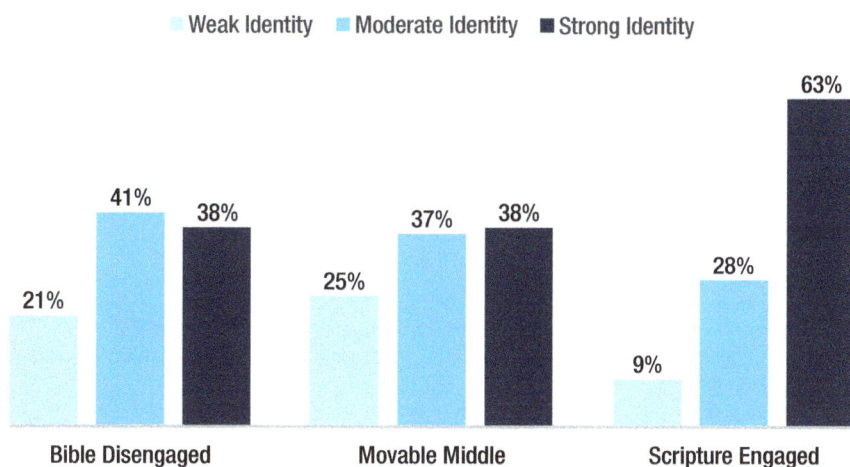

Weak Identity ■ Moderate Identity ■ Strong Identity

	Weak	Moderate	Strong
Bible Disengaged	21%	41%	38%
Movable Middle	25%	37%	38%
Scripture Engaged	9%	28%	63%

More intriguing here is the struggle of the Movable Middle. These are "sort of" Bible believers. They tend to read Scripture occasionally. It plays some part in their lives, but it's not central. They are heavily represented in those middle groups of church involvement—the Nominals and the Casuals. Some call themselves Christians but rarely attend church. Others show up, but they're not too excited about it. From a faith-and-religion standpoint, they're not sure who they are—which makes it no surprise that their Identity scores are actually a tad weaker than those of the Bible Disengaged.

The simple statistic of Bible Use has a remarkable connection to identity. People who read the Bible at least once a week are more likely to have strong Identity scores. Nearly seven of ten (69%) *daily* Bible readers are in the Strong Identity group. Yet here again we see apparent confusion in the middle. Strong Identity scores dip a bit with the once-a-month Bible readers, below all those who read the Bible more—but also below those who read it *less*. We wonder if these people want to read more often but don't get around to it, which makes them feel less confident in their faith.

Identity Levels by Bible Use Frequency

●— Weak Identity ●— Strong Identity

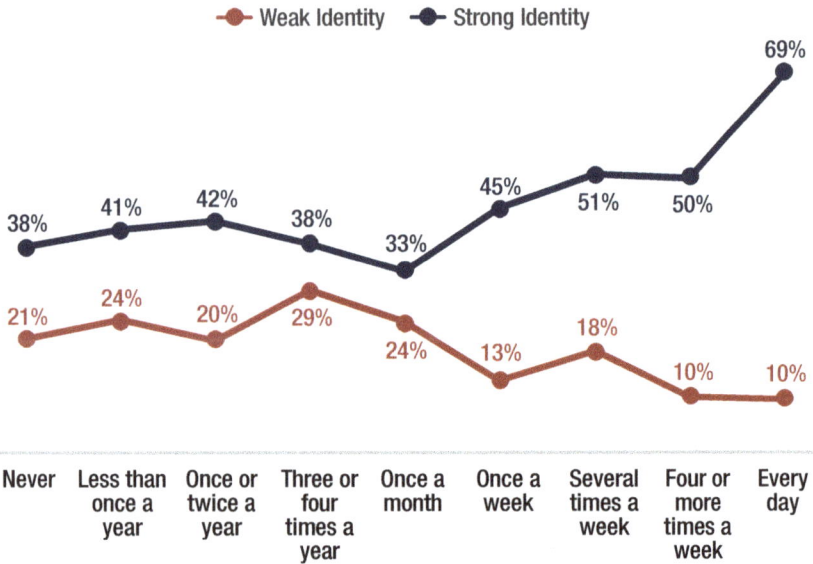

Never	Less than once a year	Once or twice a year	Three or four times a year	Once a month	Once a week	Several times a week	Four or more times a week	Every day

Strong Identity: 38%, 41%, 42%, 38%, 33%, 45%, 51%, 50%, 69%

Weak Identity: 21%, 24%, 20%, 29%, 24%, 13%, 18%, 10%, 10%

IDENTITY FACTORS IN SPIRITUAL VITALITY

Sometimes it's not *what* you say, but *how enthusiastically* you say it. This is especially true in a set of statements we presented to self-identified Christians about different aspects of spiritual growth and vitality. These include a number of "right answer" questions—where Christians know they're *supposed* to say yes—so we give them several ways to agree, from "somewhat" to "very strongly." These levels of agreement become very important as we cross-tabulate them with Identity levels.

The statement "I exist to know, love, and serve God" garners overwhelming agreement (88%), when all levels of agreement are counted. This is an identity statement, so it's no surprise that more than nine in ten Christians with Strong Identity scores agree at some level (91%). Yet even Christians at Moderate and Weak Identity levels agree at some level with this statement (84% and 86%, respectively).

The difference comes among those who agree "strongly" or "very strongly." Nearly two-thirds (64%) of Strong Identity Christians agree at this level, while far fewer of the Christians with Moderate and Weak Identity do (47% and 36%).

A similar division is seen with "I know and use my spiritual gifts to fulfill God's purposes." This could also be seen as an identity statement. In overall agreement, there's little difference among the Identity levels (83%, 78%, and 73%, high to low). But when we limit it to "strong" or "very strong" agreement, the gaps widen (42%, 23%, and 15%).

The statement "I am willing to risk everything that is important in my life for Jesus Christ" shows the same effect once again. Most Christians would see this as something they *should* agree with, and about three-quarters do. But only about a third of them give strong or very strong assent to this radical statement, and they're mostly the ones with a Strong Identity score.

Statements of Spiritual Vitality by Identity Level (and Levels of Agreement)

■ Agree Strongly or Very Strongly   ■ Agree at Any Level

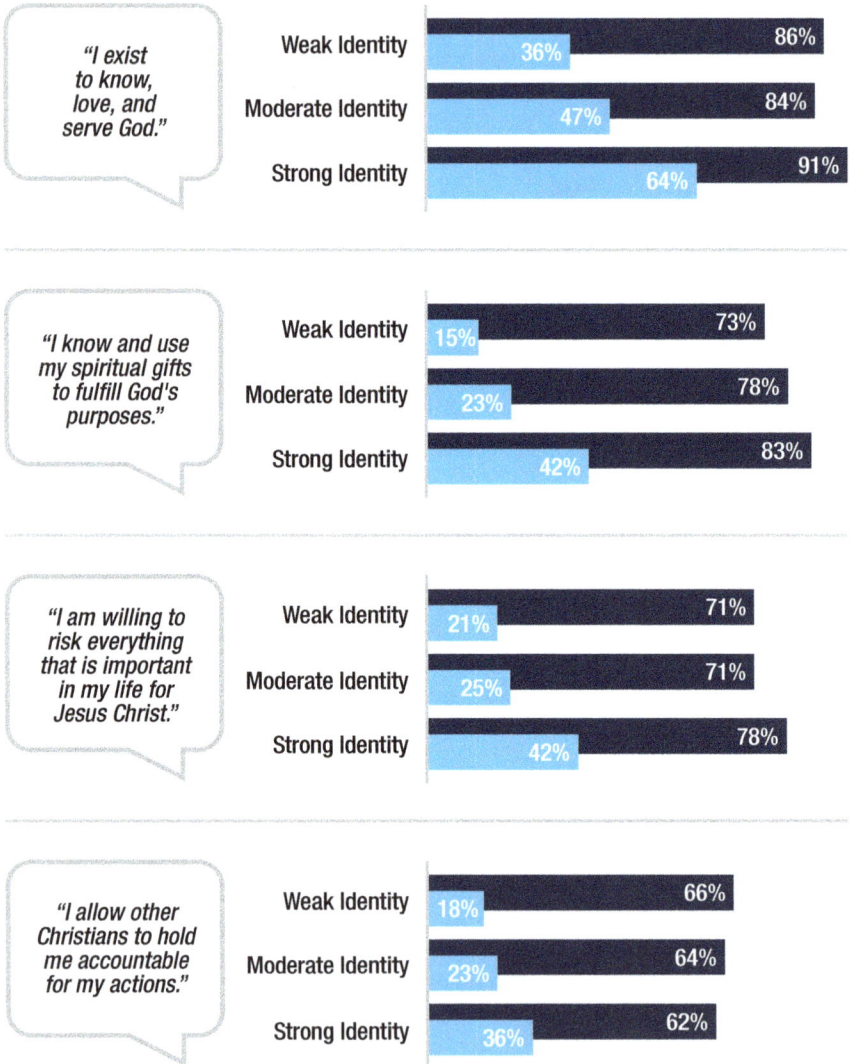

"I exist to know, love, and serve God."

	Agree Strongly or Very Strongly	Agree at Any Level
Weak Identity	36%	86%
Moderate Identity	47%	84%
Strong Identity	64%	91%

"I know and use my spiritual gifts to fulfill God's purposes."

	Agree Strongly or Very Strongly	Agree at Any Level
Weak Identity	15%	73%
Moderate Identity	23%	78%
Strong Identity	42%	83%

"I am willing to risk everything that is important in my life for Jesus Christ."

	Agree Strongly or Very Strongly	Agree at Any Level
Weak Identity	21%	71%
Moderate Identity	25%	71%
Strong Identity	42%	78%

"I allow other Christians to hold me accountable for my actions."

	Agree Strongly or Very Strongly	Agree at Any Level
Weak Identity	18%	66%
Moderate Identity	23%	64%
Strong Identity	36%	62%

Base: Self-identified Christians

We present another statement that might seem at odds with a strong sense of identity: "I allow other Christians to hold me accountable for my actions." If you know who you are, if you know what's important, what you believe and value, why should you let anyone else tell you what to do? In fact, those with low Identity scores—those who *don't* know who they are or what's important—are more likely to agree at some level with this statement. They may benefit greatly from the input of wiser believers. But when we look at the strongest levels of agreement, those at the strongest levels of Identity seem to recognize that they need the spiritual care of other Christians.

GOING FORWARD

In recent years, the *State of the Bible* report has regularly included chapters on generations, and sometimes specifically Generation Z, because that's the group everyone was worried about. One of the key issues for that group is *identity*.

This year, we have sharpened our focus to that very issue, examining how a sense of identity affects people in every generation and how it is affected by various spiritual factors. As we looked through the spiritual vitality statements, one of them caught our attention, bringing together identity with one of our favorite subjects, Bible study: "I study the Bible to know God, the truth, and to find direction for my life."

Bible Study Statement by Generation

Percent agreeing at any level

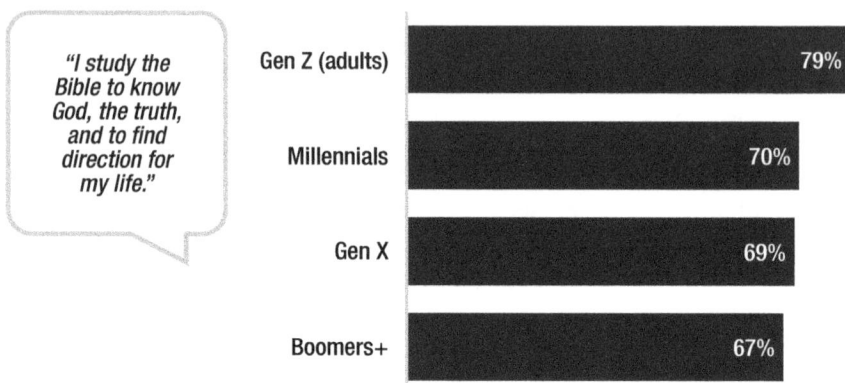

> "I study the Bible to know God, the truth, and to find direction for my life."

Generation	Percent
Gen Z (adults)	79%
Millennials	70%
Gen X	69%
Boomers+	67%

Base: Self-identified Christians

The generation of Christians that agrees most with this statement is the youngest in our survey. That makes sense, doesn't it? Most of Gen Z is at a place in life where they have big choices to make. Where will life take them? Career, education, relationships, community, development of gifts and skills—many of these 18-to-28-year-olds need direction in these matters. It's good to know they're looking into the Bible for that.

Surely there's a chorus of older Christian readers saying, "What about us? We need God's direction too!" Granted, we all need divine guidance, and we regularly find it in Scripture. Yet we hope you share our joy that nearly eight of ten Gen Z Christians are seeking direction in the Scriptures, especially at this critical time in their development.

People of every generation hear a steady thrum from our culture about who we are and who we should be. It's the core of the advertising industry—"This product is what you need to become the person you want to be." It seems we can't go thirty seconds without encountering some sort of ad hawking a car, a weight-loss drug, or a gambling site that promises to give us a new identity.

The Bible tells a different story. Let's keep listening to that. Let's keep becoming the people God wants us to be. ■

IDENTITY AND FAITH FORMATION AMONG YOUNG ADULTS

For this chapter, we interview **Dr. Arthur L. Satterwhite**, Vice President of Strategy at Young Life. He shares his on the ground ministry experience working with young people wrestling with questions of identity, faith, and coming of age.

State of the Bible
THE PODCAST

AMERICAN BIBLE SOCIETY

Identity and Faith Formation

Religious Identity vs. Practice

■ Weak Identity ■ Moderate Identity ■ Strong Identity

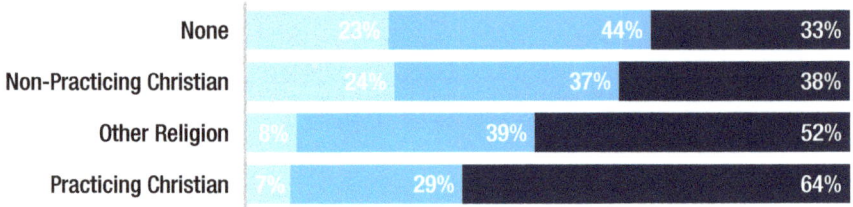

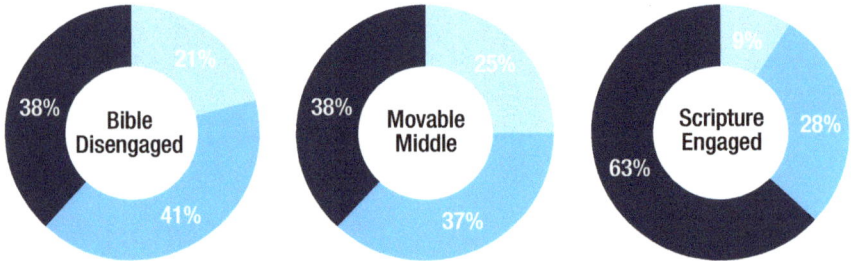

	Weak Identity	Moderate Identity	Strong Identity
None	23%	44%	33%
Non-Practicing Christian	24%	37%	38%
Other Religion	8%	39%	52%
Practicing Christian	7%	29%	64%

Bible Engagement: Identity Shaping

■ Weak Identity ■ Moderate Identity ■ Strong Identity

Bible Disengaged: 21% Weak, 41% Moderate, 38% Strong

Movable Middle: 25% Weak, 37% Moderate, 38% Strong

Scripture Engaged: 9% Weak, 28% Moderate, 63% Strong

Purpose and Identity

■ Disagree ■ Strongly or Very Strongly Agree

"I exist to know, love, and serve God."

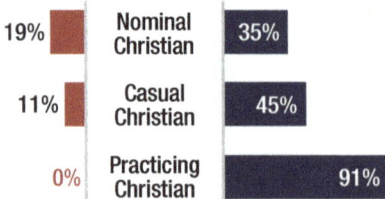

Disagree		Strongly or Very Strongly Agree
19%	Nominal Christian	35%
11%	Casual Christian	45%
0%	Practicing Christian	91%

"I study the Bible to know God, the truth, and to find direction for my life."

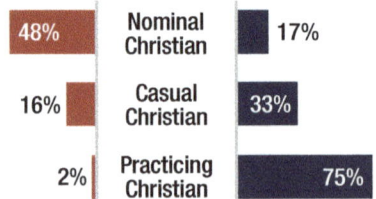

Disagree		Strongly or Very Strongly Agree
48%	Nominal Christian	17%
16%	Casual Christian	33%
2%	Practicing Christian	75%

TRUST

Many of the most pressing problems in American culture these days involve a loss of trust. We have become a suspicious people, doubting not only our social institutions, but often our neighbors and colleagues—sometimes with good reason. This trust deficit has clearly affected the nation culturally and politically, but its effect on our relationships might be just as strong, though less obvious. Might it also affect our spiritual lives?

Author Henry Cloud calls trust "the fuel for all of life. Nothing in life works without it—especially relationships. We are wired biologically, neurologically, emotionally, spiritually, and psychologically to trust. Trust is the currency that drives everything."[1]

This chapter focuses on two different types of trust: interpersonal and institutional. Do we trust the major social operations of our society—like medicine, education, and government—to do what

---

1   Cloud, H. (2023). *Trust: Knowing when to give it, when to withhold it, how to earn it, and how to fix it when it gets broken.* Worthy. Ch. 2.

they are intended to do? Also, at a personal level, do we operate in our daily lives with a degree of trust in others?

There is a wide gulf between "guarded" and "gullible." In Proverbs, a repository of practical wisdom, we find several cautions against trusting the untrustworthy (22:26, 25:19, 26:25). The Bible teaches that all humans are sinners; it's folly to think otherwise. As we present the survey results that follow, do not assume that high trust is always good and low trust bad.

Yet these numbers provide a snapshot of the American people with an interesting new filter: what or whom do we trust, and how much?

INTERPERSONAL TRUST

Our survey first asked how much people agreed (or disagreed) with five statements about trusting others. Five possible answers—from "Strongly disagree" to "Strongly agree"—were assigned values of 1 to 5.

- Most people are basically honest.
- Most people are trustworthy.
- I am trusting of others.
- Most people are sincere and well-intentioned.
- People will usually keep their promises if they make them.[2]

Overall, the average Interpersonal Trust score was close to the expected middle, at 3.2. Differences from statement to statement

---

2 Adapted from the General Trust Scale in Yamagishi, T., & Yamagishi, M. (1994). Trust and commitment in the United States and Japan. *Motivation and Emotion, 18,* 129–166. https://backend.fetzer.org/sites/default/files/images/stories/pdf/selfmeasures/Self_Measures_for_Love_and_Compassion_Research_TRUST.pdf

were minor, with most close to that overall midpoint. The one "I-statement" ("I am trusting of others") got a bit more agreement, suggesting that people like to think of themselves as trusting souls, even if they remain aware that others don't always deserve their trust.

INSTITUTIONAL TRUST

We also asked people to rate their level of trust in eight categories of social institutions —Families, Medicine, Education, Religion, Arts & Entertainment, Banking & Business, Government, and Media.[3]

Ratings started with "No Trust" (o points) and "Limited Trust" (1), extending to "Average" (2), "High" (3), and "Very High" (4) levels. Overall, combining all eight institutions, we find a mean Institutional Trust score of 1.8 on this 0–4 scale.

Social Institutions by Level of Trust

"How much do you trust each of the institutions listed below to fulfill their purpose?"

	Average Score	Percent saying "High/Very High"	Percent saying "No Trust"
Families	2.6	55%	3%
Medicine	2.2	38%	5%
Education	2.1	32%	5%
Religion	1.8	29%	17%
Arts & Entertainment	1.6	16%	15%
Banking & Business	1.6	14%	11%
Government	1.2	6%	22%
Media	1.1	5%	29%

3 We should note the timing of this survey—mid-January 2025. This was after November's election but before the Inauguration.

Families win the most trust, with well over half of respondents (55%) expressing "high" or "very high" trust. It seems we still rely on doctors and teachers, with Medicine (2.2) and Education (2.1) above the overall midpoint.

Religion (1.8) landed exactly at the average for all institutions, with its substantial level (29%) of high and very high trust balanced by an even greater number indicating "no trust" or "limited trust" (41% combined). Apparently religion evokes a sort of love/hate response, or at least trust/distrust. There's less middle ground.

Readers will not be surprised in today's culture that Government (1.2) and Media (1.1) receive the least trust, with about a quarter of Americans (22%, 29%) not trusting them at all.

DEMOGRAPHICS

Do some groups of people express more trust in other people? How do age, education, income, or other demographics affect which institutions people trust or how trusting they are in general?[4]

EDUCATION AND INCOME

You might assume that highly educated people are trained to be skeptics. Perhaps, but Interpersonal Trust scores *rise* with greater education. Though the "high trust" group includes only a quarter of all Americans, it has nearly four of ten (39%) of those who have

---

4 For Interpersonal Trust scores, we divided responders into three groups—low, moderate, and high—with roughly half of respondents in the moderate group and a quarter in each of the extremes. Low Trust (22% of the public) includes average per-question scores of 1.0 to 2.4; Moderate Trust (53%) is 2.5 to 3.9; High Trust (25%) is 4.0 to 5.0.

post-college study and nearly three of ten (29%) with just college degrees. Those with only high school diplomas have the highest number in the "low trust" group (27%).

Interpersonal Trust by Education

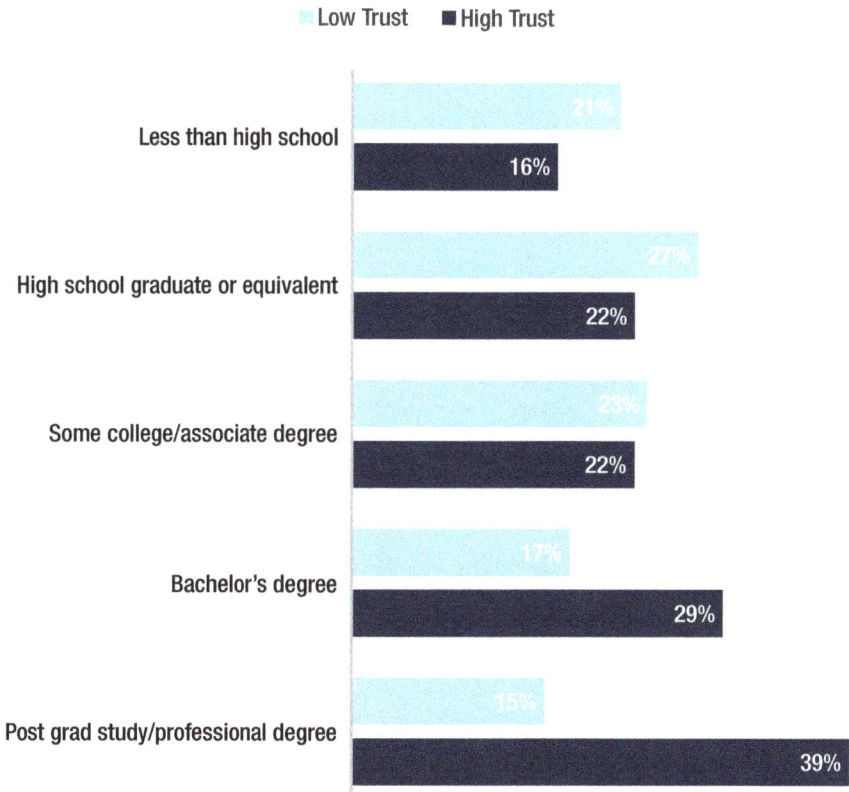

Low Trust   High Trust

Education	Low Trust	High Trust
Less than high school	21%	16%
High school graduate or equivalent	27%	22%
Some college/associate degree	23%	22%
Bachelor's degree	17%	29%
Post grad study/professional degree	15%	39%

A person's level of education also makes a difference in Institutional Trust. We see this especially with medical and educational institutions. Those with college degrees show greater trust in those fields, and those with graduate degrees even more so. Those with less education are more apt to trust religious institutions. Trust in families rises with each level of education.

Institutional Trust by Education

"How much do you trust each of the institutions listed below to fulfill their purpose?"

	Less than HS	HS grad or equiv.	Some college/ associate degree	Bachelor's degree	Post grad study/ professional degree	Total
Families	2.4	2.5	2.6	2.7	2.8	2.6
Medicine	2.0	2.0	2.2	2.3	2.5	2.2
Education	2.1	1.8	2.1	2.2	2.4	2.1
Religion	1.7	2.0	1.9	1.6	1.7	1.8
Arts & Entertainment	1.8	1.5	1.5	1.7	1.7	1.6
Banking & Business	1.7	1.6	1.5	1.6	1.7	1.6
Government	1.3	1.1	1.2	1.3	1.5	1.2
Media	1.2	1.1	1.0	1.1	1.1	1.1

Scale: 0–4

This is also a case where income levels reflect education levels. People with higher incomes tend to report more trust in the institutions of Families, Medicine, and Education—and less trust in Religion.

GENERATIONS

Interpersonally, older generations trust people more than younger generations. You might expect battle-hardened cynicism among seniors and naïve optimism in our youngest adults, but that's not what we find. In our high–moderate–low tally of different age groups, more than a third (36%) of the Boomer+ generation shows high Interpersonal Trust, and only one in eight (13%) are in the low-trust group. Generation Z has significantly more representation in the low-trust group (26%) than in the high-trust group (18%), and the same is true of Millennials (27%, 19%).

Interpersonal Trust by Generation

■ Gen Z (adults)   ■ Millennials   ■ Gen X   ■ Boomers+

	Low Trust	High Trust
Gen Z (adults)	26%	18%
Millennials	27%	19%
Gen X	23%	24%
Boomers+	13%	36%

With regard to Institutional Trust, the generations do not vary greatly. Generation Z is the most likely group to trust in Arts & Entertainment. The Boomer+ generation declares trust for Medicine and Religion more than younger generations do.

Our numbers on education, income, and generation track closely with a recent survey from the Pew Research Center, which used an interpersonal trust question similar to some of ours. Since they had asked the same question in 2020, they were able to compare the data over time, and they found a significant decrease in trust. As possible causes, Pew cites political polarization, increasing internet use (which might reduce real-life connections), greater ethnic diversity, and religious decline.[5]

TRUST AND SCRIPTURE ENGAGEMENT

The Bible is blunt about the sinful state of humanity. "The heart is deceitful above all things and beyond cure," moans Jeremiah (17:9 NIV). "There is no one righteous, not even one," writes Paul, as he launches a barrage of quotations from the Psalms to support the charge (Romans 3:10 NIV).

So we might expect Scripture Engaged people to balk at the trust statements we offered, especially "Most people are basically honest." But they didn't. Despite any theological misgivings, the Scripture Engaged scored significantly higher in Interpersonal Trust than the Movable Middle and the Bible Disengaged.

---

5 Silver, L., et al. (2025). Americans' trust in one another. Pew Research Center. https://www.pewresearch.org/2025/05/08/americans-trust-in-one-another/

Of course the Bible also teaches about God's remarkable love for sinful humanity and our responsibility to love others—even if they're strangers, even if they're enemies. It appears that many of those who read and apply the Scriptures are trying to practice Christian love by thinking the best of people, by giving them the benefit of the doubt, by trusting them.

Interpersonal Trust by Scripture Engagement

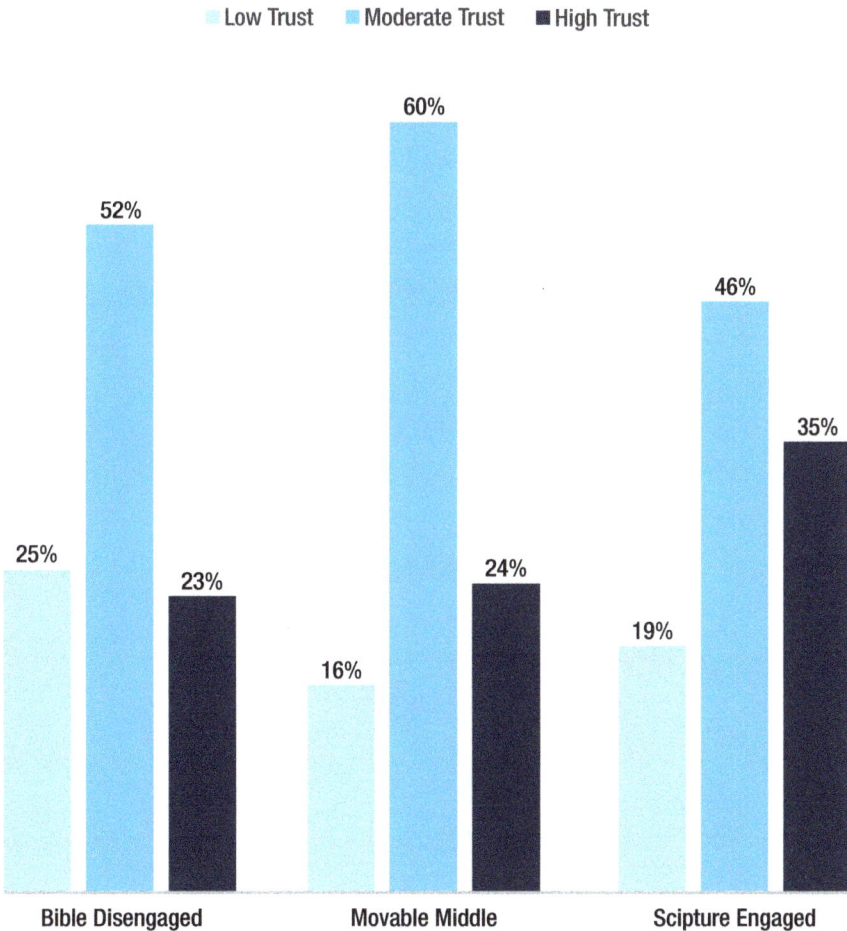

Low Trust   Moderate Trust   High Trust

	Low Trust	Moderate Trust	High Trust
Bible Disengaged	25%	52%	23%
Movable Middle	16%	60%	24%
Scipture Engaged	19%	46%	35%

Institutional Trust by Scripture Engagement

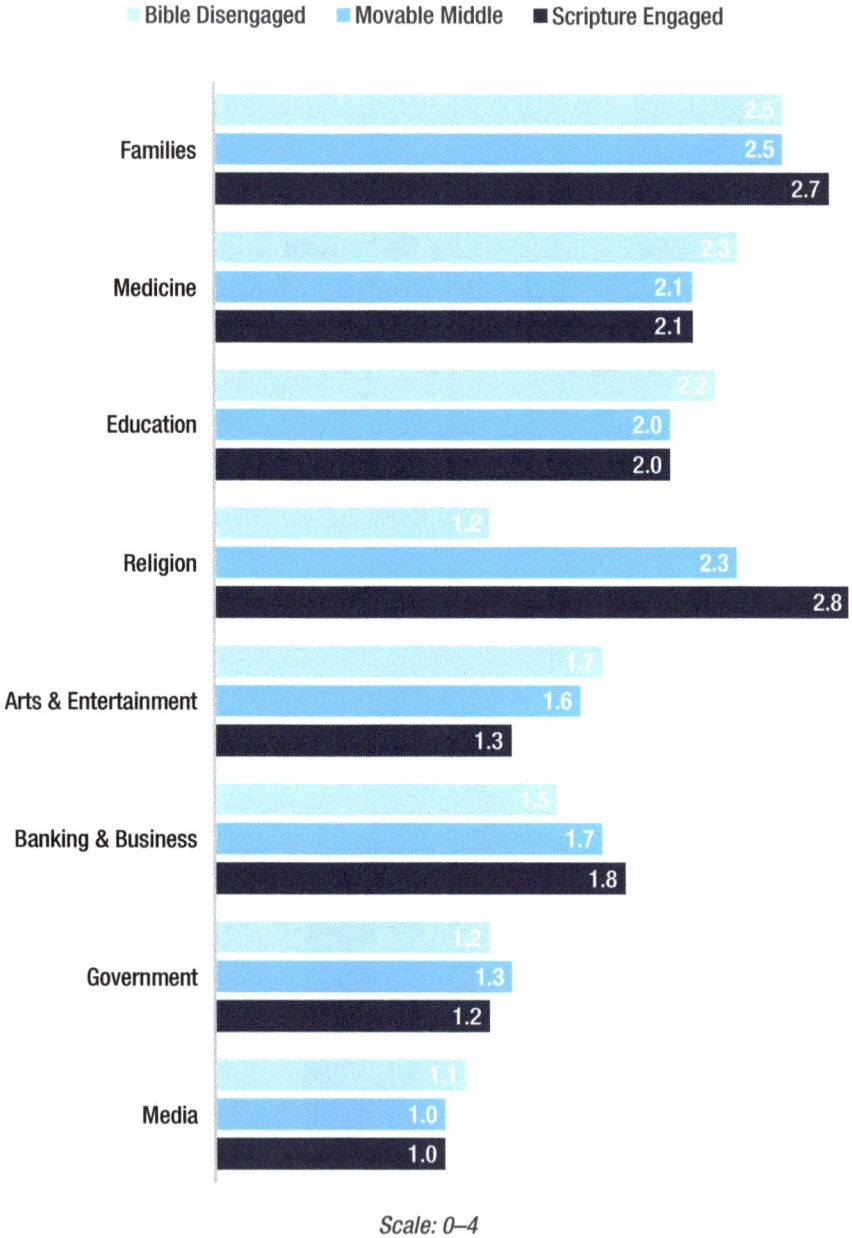

Bible Disengaged ■ Movable Middle ■ Scripture Engaged

Families
- Bible Disengaged: 2.5
- Movable Middle: 2.5
- Scripture Engaged: 2.7

Medicine
- Bible Disengaged: 2.3
- Movable Middle: 2.1
- Scripture Engaged: 2.1

Education
- Bible Disengaged: 2.2
- Movable Middle: 2.0
- Scripture Engaged: 2.0

Religion
- Bible Disengaged: 1.2
- Movable Middle: 2.3
- Scripture Engaged: 2.8

Arts & Entertainment
- Bible Disengaged: 1.7
- Movable Middle: 1.6
- Scripture Engaged: 1.3

Banking & Business
- Bible Disengaged: 1.5
- Movable Middle: 1.7
- Scripture Engaged: 1.8

Government
- Bible Disengaged: 1.2
- Movable Middle: 1.3
- Scripture Engaged: 1.2

Media
- Bible Disengaged: 1.1
- Movable Middle: 1.0
- Scripture Engaged: 1.0

Scale: 0–4

This high level of trust does *not* carry over to institutions. As you might expect, the Scripture Engaged show the highest level of trust in Religion (2.8 out of a possible 4) and Families (2.7). Curiously, they also lead the pack in trusting Banking & Business (1.8). Yet they are significantly lower than the Movable Middle and Bible Disengaged in their trust of Arts & Entertainment (1.3). Remember that one of the questions determining Scripture engagement involves the Bible's influence on "the movies and television I choose to watch."

POLITICAL IDENTIFICATION

State of the Bible seldom features political findings given our focus on Scripture. Yet political identification is pertinent in this chapter. *Where people place their trust* could be the most telling difference between the two major U.S. parties. The difference also affects many aspects of life in our country, in our communities, and even in our churches. Scripture Engagement also plays a pivotal role.

With half (50%) agreeing or strongly agreeing on the five Interpersonal Trust statements, Democrats are more trusting than Republicans (43%). Both score far higher than Independents (30%).

Where people place their trust could be the most telling difference between the two major U.S. parties.

Institutional Trust by Political Affiliation

"How much do you trust each of the institutions listed below to fulfill their purpose?"

	Democrat	Lean Democrat	Independent/ None	Lean Republican	Republican
Families	2.6	2.5	2.4	2.7	2.7
Medicine	2.6	2.5	1.9	2.0	2.0
Education	2.5	2.4	1.8	1.8	1.7
Religion	1.6	1.1	1.6	2.1	2.2
Arts & Entertainment	1.9	2.0	1.5	1.4	1.2
Banking & Business	1.7	1.4	1.5	1.7	1.7
Government	1.4	1.2	1.1	1.0	1.1
Media	1.4	1.2	0.9	0.8	0.8

Scale: 0–4

We see clear differences in Institutional Trust. Republicans are slightly more likely to trust the institution of Families, and considerably more trusting of Religion. Democrats are far more likely to trust the institutions of Medicine and Education. The two parties are rather even when it comes to trusting Banking & Business, with Democrats having somewhat more trust in Government, Media, and Arts & Entertainment.

POLITICS, TRUST, AND SCRIPTURE ENGAGEMENT

As we've seen, Democrats are more trusting than Republicans, with regard to Interpersonal Trust, but that difference occurs mostly among the Bible Disengaged. Among Republicans who are Scripture Engaged, the personal trust level is nearly equal to that of Scripture Engaged Democrats.

Interpersonal Trust by Political Affiliation and Scripture Engagement

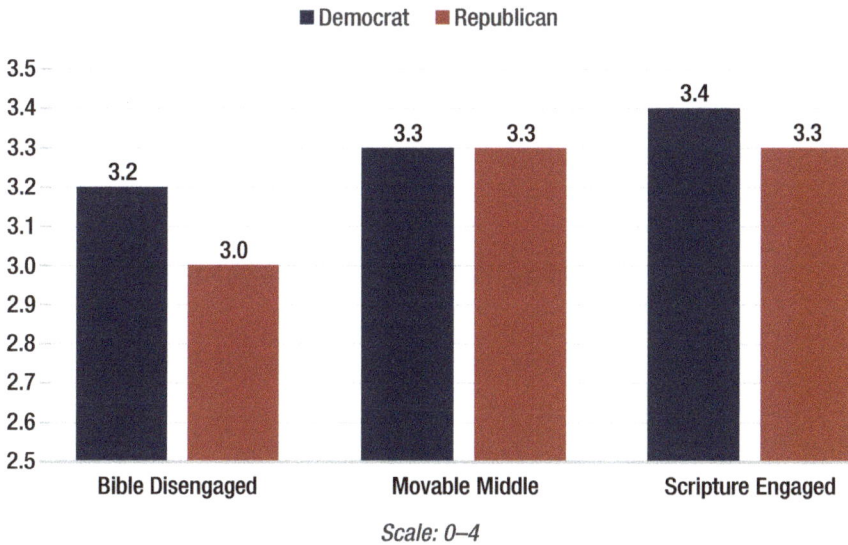

■ Democrat ■ Republican

	Bible Disengaged	Movable Middle	Scripture Engaged
Democrat	3.2	3.3	3.4
Republican	3.0	3.3	3.3

Scale: 0–4

Moving to Institutional Trust, several findings stand out.

- Trust in **Families** is quite high in both parties, and highest among the Scripture Engaged.
- There's a much wider variation with trust in **Religion**. As we might expect, levels of Scripture Engagement parallel the levels of institutional trust in Religion. Yet the difference from bottom to top is much greater among Democrats. Bible Disengaged Democrats trust Religion less than any of the seven other institutions in this survey, while Scripture Engaged Democrats trust Religion more than any other.

Institutional Trust by Political Affiliation and Scripture Engagement (Selected Categories)

Legend:
- Democrat Bible Disengaged
- Democrat Movable Middle
- Democrat Scripture Engaged
- Republican Bible Disengaged
- Republican Movable Middle
- Republican Scripture Engaged

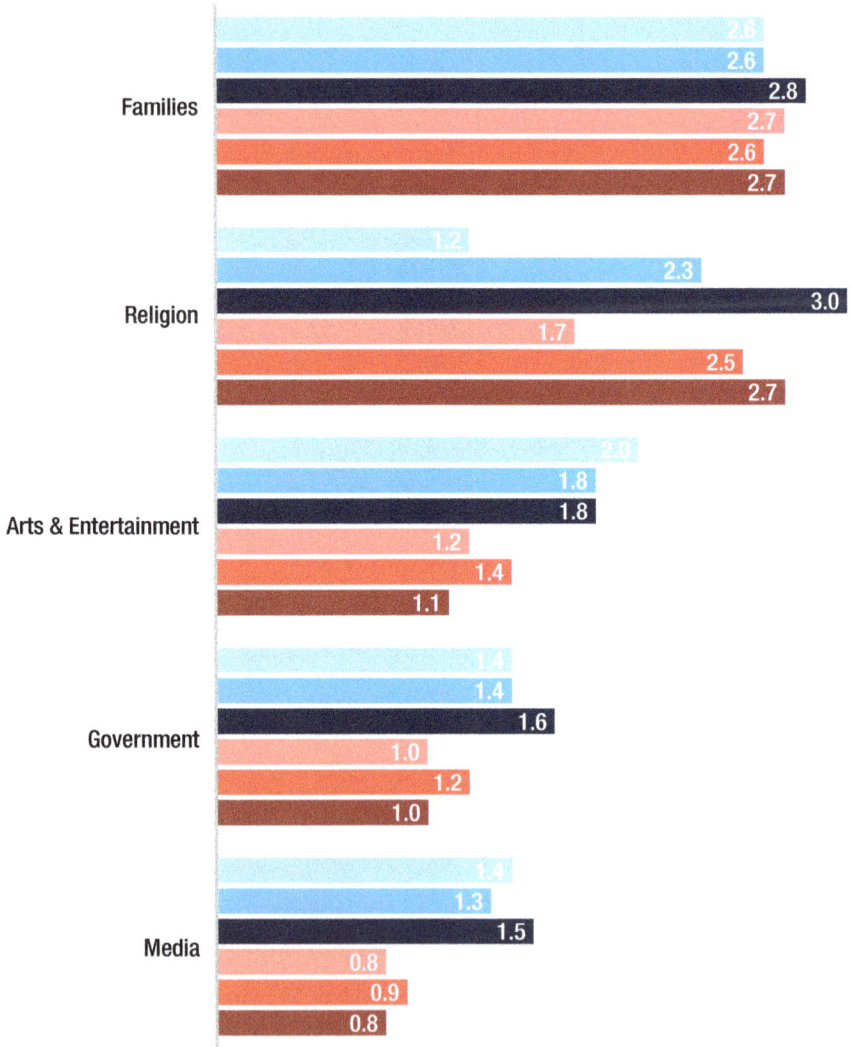

Families
- Democrat Bible Disengaged: 2.6
- Democrat Movable Middle: 2.6
- Democrat Scripture Engaged: 2.8
- Republican Bible Disengaged: 2.7
- Republican Movable Middle: 2.6
- Republican Scripture Engaged: 2.7

Religion
- Democrat Bible Disengaged: 1.2
- Democrat Movable Middle: 2.3
- Democrat Scripture Engaged: 3.0
- Republican Bible Disengaged: 1.7
- Republican Movable Middle: 2.5
- Republican Scripture Engaged: 2.7

Arts & Entertainment
- Democrat Bible Disengaged: 2.0
- Democrat Movable Middle: 1.8
- Democrat Scripture Engaged: 1.8
- Republican Bible Disengaged: 1.2
- Republican Movable Middle: 1.4
- Republican Scripture Engaged: 1.1

Government
- Democrat Bible Disengaged: 1.4
- Democrat Movable Middle: 1.4
- Democrat Scripture Engaged: 1.6
- Republican Bible Disengaged: 1.0
- Republican Movable Middle: 1.2
- Republican Scripture Engaged: 1.0

Media
- Democrat Bible Disengaged: 1.4
- Democrat Movable Middle: 1.3
- Democrat Scripture Engaged: 1.5
- Republican Bible Disengaged: 0.8
- Republican Movable Middle: 0.9
- Republican Scripture Engaged: 0.8

Scale: 0–4

- While Republicans in general put less trust in the institution of **Arts & Entertainment**, in both parties the Scripture Engaged show less trust than the Bible Disengaged.
- That's not the case with **Government** or **Media**, where the highest level of trust is seen in Scripture Engaged Democrats.

TRUST, TRAUMA, AND FORGIVENESS

Trust is often a casualty of trauma. People who have suffered greatly, especially at the hands of other people, naturally find trust more difficult. We know this anecdotally, but do we have statistics to back it up? And just how serious is the problem?

Nearly half of Americans (46%) have "experienced or witnessed physical, psychological or emotional trauma." Three-quarters of these (36% of Americans) have experienced trauma themselves, while some have just witnessed it.

The vast majority (89%) of those who have experienced or witnessed trauma say they still feel its effects, at least "sometimes." More than a third of them (35%) say "about half the time" or more. Pause a moment to take this in. Past trauma continues to plague people far into the future. More than a quarter of Americans (27%)—people in your community, your workplace, your church—rate the continuing effects of past trauma "moderate" to "overwhelming" (at least 4 on a 0–10 scale).

Trauma in the U.S.

"Have you ever experienced or witnessed physical, psychological or emotional trauma?"

46%
of American
adults have
experienced or
witnessed trauma

*(36%
experienced it
and 10% only
witnessed it)*

Of the 46% who have witnessed or
experienced trauma, it still affects . . .

10% Always (5% of Americans)	12% Most of the time (6% of Americans)	13% About half the time (6% of Americans)	54% Sometimes (25% of Americans)	11% Never (5% of Americans)

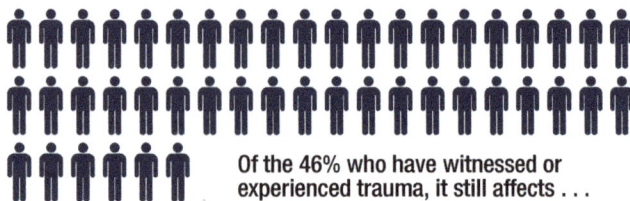

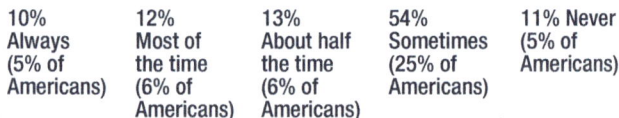

89% at least "sometimes" (42% of Americans)

54%
of American
adults have not
experienced or
witnessed
trauma

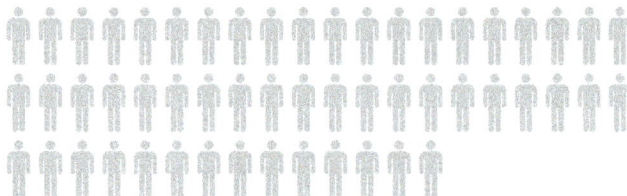

Of the 46% who have witnessed
or experienced trauma, how
much does it affect them now?

*They were asked to rate the
severity of the trauma effects
(e.g., anxiety, crying spells,
depression, sleep disturbance,
etc.) they were experiencing
on a scale of 0 to 10.*

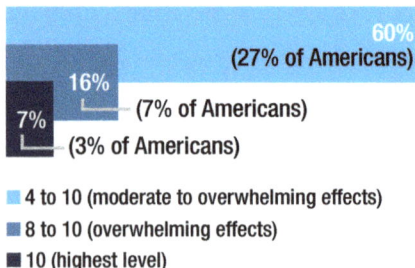

60%
(27% of Americans)

16%
(7% of Americans)

7%
(3% of Americans)

- 4 to 10 (moderate to overwhelming effects)
- 8 to 10 (overwhelming effects)
- 10 (highest level)

Can we say definitively that trauma damages trust? Yes, with certain types of trauma. For those who have suffered "the violent/sudden death of a friend" or a natural disaster, the effect on their Interpersonal Trust score is minimal, nearly non-existent. In the case of "life-threatening illness/injury," people actually score higher in Interpersonal Trust, suggesting that perhaps they have learned to depend on other helpful people.

The three types of trauma that damage trust are **assault, abuse,** and **unwanted sexual contact**. These traumatic events all happen at the hands of other people, often people whom the sufferer knows and perhaps has trusted. For people who rate the continuing effects of these traumatic events "moderate" to "overwhelming," there's a significant drop in Interpersonal Trust.

"One of the symptoms of trauma is reliving the experience in nightmares or flashbacks," says Rebecca Taguma, Senior Director of Restoring Hope at American Bible Society. "So, when someone has experienced trauma, naturally their trust is eroded, because they're reminded constantly of this really painful thing that happened. And if they're avoiding reminders, they don't want to reestablish relationships with the person or the place involved in the trauma. It becomes a barrier to connection with others."

Can we say definitively that trauma damages trust? Yes, with certain types of trauma.

Interpersonal Trust Among Those Suffering Moderate to Overwhelming Effects of Certain Traumas

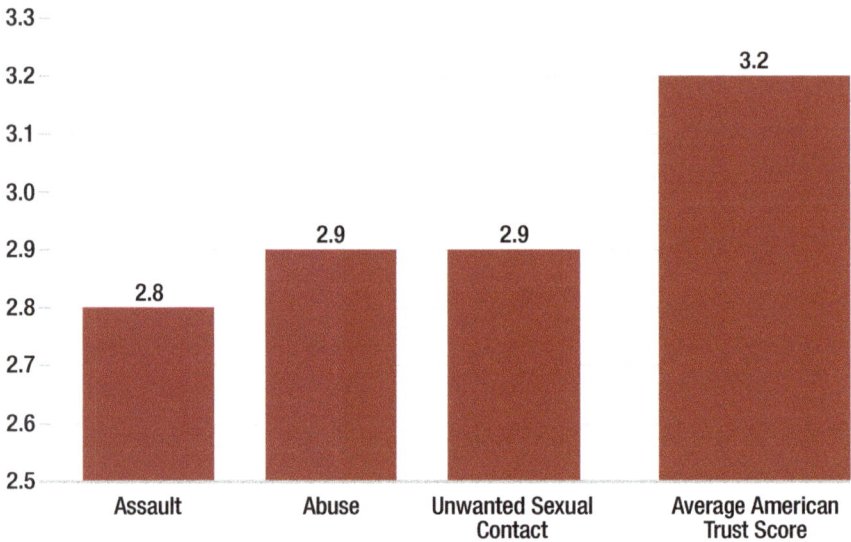

Scale: 0–4

FORGIVENESS

Our survey also asks whether people agree or disagree with the statement "I am able to sincerely forgive whatever someone else has done to me, regardless of whether they ever ask for forgiveness or not." Nearly two-thirds of all respondents (66%) agree, at least somewhat, though we suspect that's easier to say than do.

Trauma survivors often need to travel a long, hard road toward forgiveness. Volumes have been written on what forgiveness is and isn't; it's a worthy study. Yet we find that the ability to forgive is connected to higher levels of interpersonal trust. Just as trauma damages trust, forgiveness may restore it.

"Healing is a process that takes time," says Taguma, "and forgiveness is often a critical part of that journey. It can't be forced, but when it happens, the freedom that comes is beautiful. When we can actually forgive those who have done us wrong, the impact is not only our ability to trust ourselves and others, but it frees our spirit, mind, and body to have new life and hope."[6]

Levels of Interpersonal Trust by Ability to Forgive

"I am able to sincerely forgive whatever someone else has done to me, regardless of whether they ever ask for forgiveness or not."

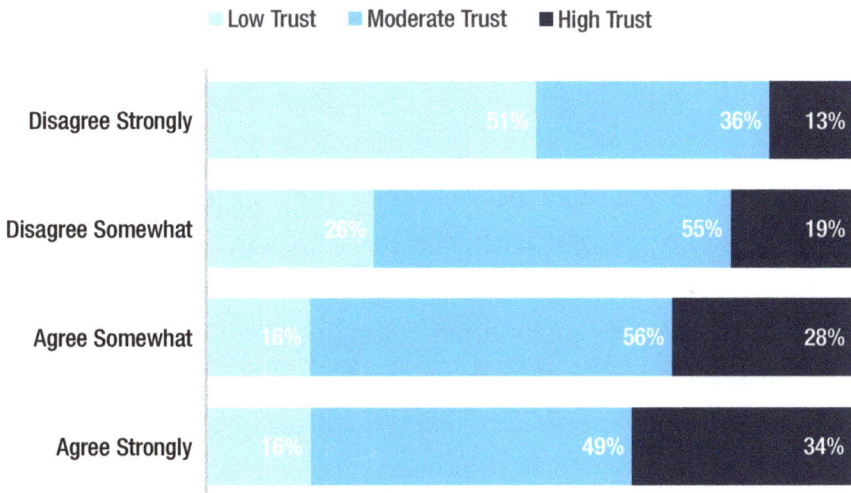

Low Trust Moderate Trust High Trust

	Low Trust	Moderate Trust	High Trust
Disagree Strongly	51%	36%	13%
Disagree Somewhat	26%	55%	19%
Agree Somewhat	16%	56%	28%
Agree Strongly	16%	49%	34%

Remember that only one in four (25%) of the general public are in the High Trust group, but when people agree strongly that they're able to forgive others, that rises to one in three (34%). Meanwhile, among those who disagree strongly, only one in eight (13%) are in the High Trust group, compared to more than half (51%) wallowing in Low Trust.

6 Taguma, R. (2025). Personal interview. https://www.americanbible.org/restoringhope

FORGIVENESS AND HEALING

Restoring Hope is the healing and resilience ministry of American Bible Society.

Visit us at **americanbible.org/restoringhope** to find free resources for church leaders who care for hurting people.

RESTORING
HOPE

Even among those who have suffered interpersonal traumas of assault, abuse, or unwanted sexual contact, we see that those who say they are able to forgive have trust levels on par with the average American—and in some cases, higher.

TRUSTING IN THE BIBLE

We've been examining trust in various contexts. Institutions may or may not deserve our trust, and the same can be said of people. Whether or not we choose to count on our local bank or our shifty brother-in-law, we can confidently put our trust in the Lord. And we consistently invite others to trust him, too. (Some of our readers may have had the words of Proverbs 3:5 wafting through their minds: "Trust in the LORD with all your heart.")

Those of us who seek to share the Bible's life-changing message often encounter a trust problem. When we quote powerful Scriptures, it's not unusual to hear, "Why should I believe that? Kahlil Gibran and Oprah and this wannabe Internet influencer say inspiring things too."

So, before we leave the subject of trust, we turn to people's views on the reliability of the Bible. Several questions in our survey provide insight.

Various Views of Trust in the Bible

"The Bible is totally accurate in all the principles it presents."

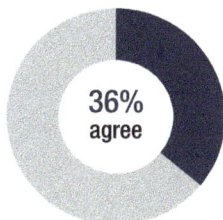

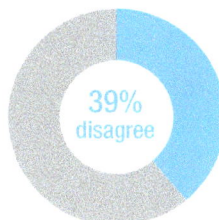

36% agree

39% disagree

"The Bible is just another book of teachings written by people that contains stories and advice."

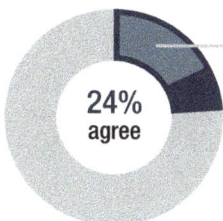

24% agree

Three-quarters of that 24% (thus 18% of the public) feel "The Bible was written to control or manipulate other people."

"The message of the Bible has transformed my life."

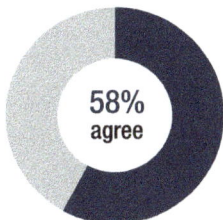

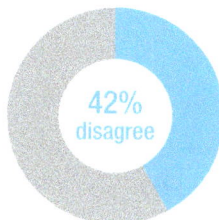

58% agree

42% disagree

"The Bible is totally accurate in all the principles it presents." Elsewhere in the poll we have questions that draw out people's views on a doctrine of biblical inspiration, but this is a more general statement of reliability. More than a third (36%) agree, either strongly or somewhat. A few more (39%) disagree at some level, with the rest undecided. Keep this in mind as you take your message to the public square. About a third of those listeners will trust what the Bible has to say. Others will be undecided or skeptical.

"The Bible is just another book of teachings written by people that contains stories and advice." This is one of those doctrine-of-inspiration questions. We wanted to gauge the level of skepticism in our society. While this statement is not especially negative, it has no sense of the divine origin or power of Scripture. About a quarter of the public (24%) agree with this statement.

"The Bible was written to control or manipulate other people." This was a follow-up for those who say the Bible is "just another book." At this point we move from a lack of trust to active mistrust. These people don't just ignore God's hand in Scripture, they object to the control and manipulation they assume lies behind it. Three-quarters of the "just another book" people (18% of the public) agree with this statement.

It may be important for us to see this spiritual topography of our culture. Sometimes it can feel as if no one trusts the Bible anymore. Public discourse and the media can lead us to assume that a vast majority write off the Bible as a manipulative fraud. But more than a third trust in the accuracy of biblical principles. Only a quarter see the Bible as "just another book," and less than a fifth feel it was written to "control or manipulate." We mourn for that 18 percent, we can pray for their hearts to soften, and we can engage in conversations that lovingly challenge their assumptions. Yet we need not fear that this is the majority opinion in our society.

Trust in the Bible is more than an intellectual affirmation of ideas *about* it, but a life-changing interaction with the God who speaks through it, so we looked at one more item in our survey.

"The message of the Bible has transformed my life." You might be surprised and heartened to know that well over half of the respondents (58%) agree. They might define those terms in various ways, they may understand the message differently, the transformation might be big or small, but these people, representing 148 million American adults, are willing to say on a survey that they've been changed by the Bible's message.

The Christian life is built on trust—not just in the words we read on a page or screen, but in the God who communicates with us and transforms us, sustaining us with his powerful Word, especially in those times when we need him most. ◾

TRUST, TRAUMA, AND FORGIVENESS

Dr. Henry Cloud, bestselling author, leadership expert, and clinical psychologist, offers viewers and listeners a seasoned perspective on the intersection of trust, trauma, faith, and the Bible.

State of the Bible
THE PODCAST

AMERICAN BIBLE SOCIETY

Does America Trust the Bible?

"The Bible is totally accurate in all the principles it presents."

BIBLE

36% agree

26% neither agree nor disagree

39% disagree

Distrust Among the Non-Religious

25% of Americans are religious "Nones," claiming no religion

60% of Nones believe the Bible is "just another book of teachings written by people that contains stories and advice."

50% of Nones believe the Bible was written to control or manipulate other people.

Trust in the Bible by Faith Participation Level

"The Bible is totally accurate in all the principles it presents."

■ Disagree ■ Agree

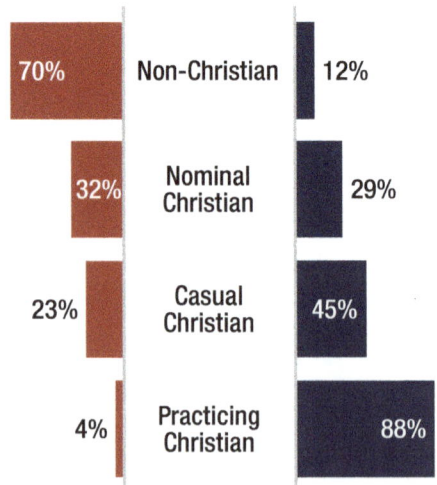

	Disagree	Agree
Non-Christian	70%	12%
Nominal Christian	32%	29%
Casual Christian	23%	45%
Practicing Christian	4%	88%

CHAPTER 8

LOVE AND GENEROSITY

"The command that Christ has given us is this: whoever loves God must love others also" (1 John 4:21). The Bible teems with challenges like this. Some preachers talk about the vertical and horizontal aspects of the Christian faith, and that's a helpful visual reference, but the truth is far more all-encompassing. God isn't just "up there"—he's with us and within us and loving others through us. Our relationship with God is inextricably connected with how we act toward others.

The centerpiece of *State of the Bible* research is Scripture engagement—not only reading the Bible but living out its teachings. Several questions measure the impact of Scripture reading on people's relationships with God and others, including these:

> *As a result of using the Bible, within the past month, I show more loving behavior towards others.*
>
> *As a result of using the Bible, within the past month, I am more generous with my time, energy, or financial resources.*

The survey asks how much people agree or disagree with these statements.

Loving Behavior by Faith Participation Level[1][2]

*"As a result of using the Bible, within the past month,
I show more loving behavior towards others."*

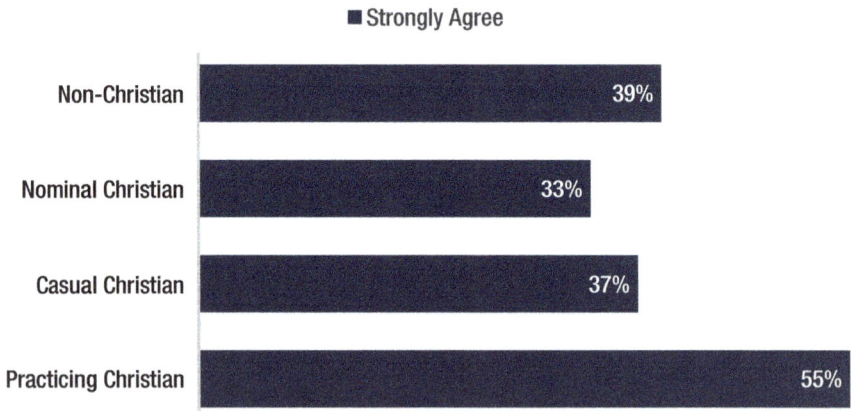

■ Strongly Agree

Non-Christian	39%
Nominal Christian	33%
Casual Christian	37%
Practicing Christian	55%

Base: Those who have used the Bible in the past month

---

1 The Non-Christian group, 36% of the American public, includes Jews, Jehovah's Witnesses, Mormons, and others who do not claim Christianity. This reflects responses from people who have read the Bible in the past month.
2 "Strongly Agree" includes those who agree "Strongly" and "Very Strongly." This will be the case throughout this chapter.

As we might expect, Practicing Christians (who attend church in person or online at least once a month and consider their faith very important to them) report significantly more biblical impact on their lives, leading to "more loving behavior" (55% strongly agree). Among Casual and Nominal Christians, only about a third indicate strong agreement (37% and 33%). In fact, among the Non-Christians who have read the Bible in the past month (a small group), the level of strong agreement is slightly higher (39%).

Generosity by Faith Participation Level

"As a result of using the Bible, within the past month, I am more generous with my time, energy or financial resources."

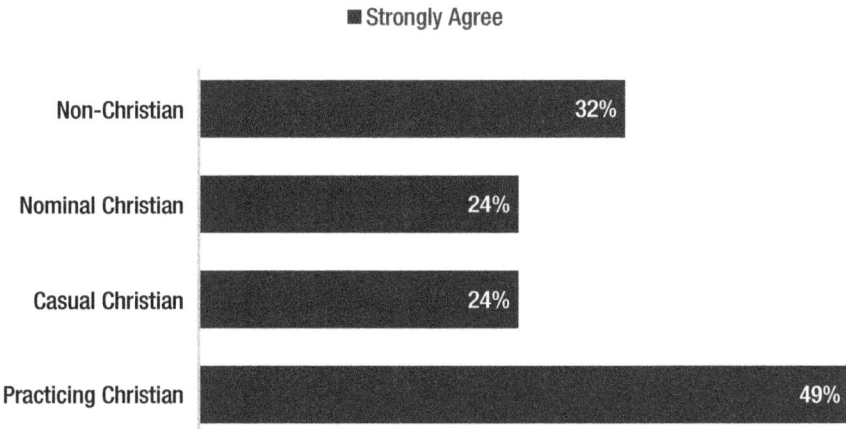

■ Strongly Agree

Non-Christian	32%
Nominal Christian	24%
Casual Christian	24%
Practicing Christian	49%

Base: Those who have used the Bible in the past month

We find a similar story with regard to the second theme of this chapter, generosity. About half of Practicing Christians (49%) strongly agree that the Bible leads them to be more generous, twice the level of Casual or Nominal Christians (both 24%). Nearly a third of Non-Christians who have read the Bible in the past month (32%) strongly agree that it increases their generosity.

More than half of Christians—and non-Christians who read it—say that loving behavior and increased generosity result from their interaction with the Bible.

These data points reaffirm what we've been saying for seven chapters already: *The Bible has impact.* And it is positive impact. More than half of Christians—and non-Christians who read it—agree on some level that loving behavior and increased generosity result from their interaction with the Bible. These findings also confirm that those who are more committed in their faith are more likely to experience the Bible's impact in these areas. The Bible can still affect you, even if your faith isn't very important to you or if you seldom attend church. But if you're serious about encountering God in Scripture, you're likely to exhibit some serious changes in your life.

PRO-SOCIAL ATTITUDES

For several years now, our survey has included questions about particular "pro-social behaviors." We recognize that some of them are now hot-button issues in our culture, but the Bible addresses these matters. Questions of *how* and *why* and *how much* will likely remain contentious, but we wondered how Christians process the biblical teaching.

The survey asks how much people agree or disagree:

It is important for me to . . .

- *Welcome immigrants into my community*
- *Befriend people of other races*
- *Befriend people of other religions*
- *Care for the environment*
- *Advocate for those who are oppressed by society*

Pro-Social Attitudes, 2022–2025

Percent who "strongly" or "very strongly" agree

■ 2022   ■ 2023   ■ 2024   ■ 2025

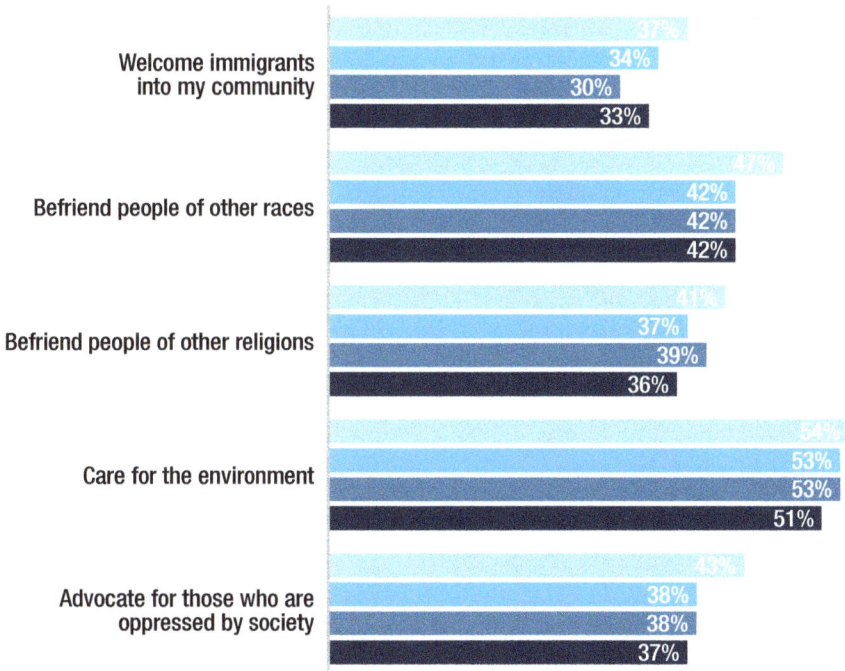

Welcome immigrants into my community
- 37%
- 34%
- 30%
- 33%

Befriend people of other races
- 47%
- 42%
- 42%
- 42%

Befriend people of other religions
- 41%
- 37%
- 39%
- 36%

Care for the environment
- 54%
- 53%
- 53%
- 51%

Advocate for those who are oppressed by society
- 43%
- 38%
- 38%
- 37%

Surveys were conducted in January of each year.

Overall, we see a slight move downward. We're dealing with a few percentage points year by year, so it's not a major lurch in public opinion. But, among all Americans, the level of strong agreement has grown decidedly weaker on all five issues between 2022 and 2025.

Does Scripture Engagement make any difference here? Bible-believing Christians often differ with each other on the details of how society should address these types of issues (or how to define terms like *welcome, care,* and *oppressed),* but do they show a collective commitment to these broad statements of love and support?

Pro-Social Attitudes by Scripture Engagement, 2025

Percent who "strongly" or "very strongly" agree

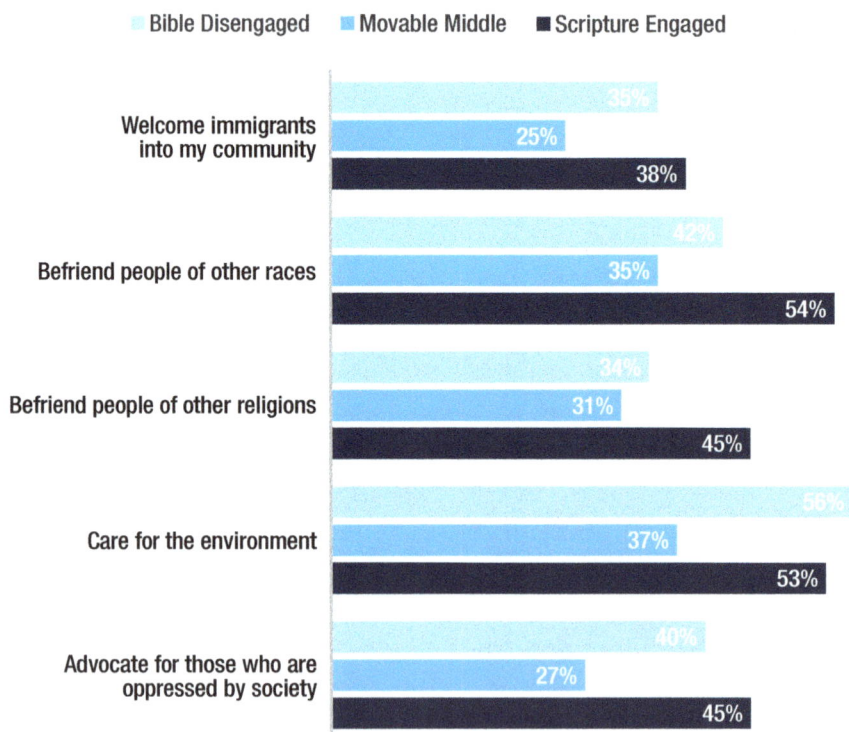

Bible Disengaged ■ Movable Middle ■ Scripture Engaged

Welcome immigrants into my community
- Bible Disengaged: 35%
- Movable Middle: 25%
- Scripture Engaged: 38%

Befriend people of other races
- Bible Disengaged: 42%
- Movable Middle: 35%
- Scripture Engaged: 54%

Befriend people of other religions
- Bible Disengaged: 34%
- Movable Middle: 31%
- Scripture Engaged: 45%

Care for the environment
- Bible Disengaged: 56%
- Movable Middle: 37%
- Scripture Engaged: 53%

Advocate for those who are oppressed by society
- Bible Disengaged: 40%
- Movable Middle: 27%
- Scripture Engaged: 45%

Yes, Scripture Engaged people show the highest levels of agreement on most of these pro-social issues, with the greatest differences occurring on the questions of befriending people of other races or religions. Only on the environmental question do the Scripture Engaged (53%) fall behind the Bible Disengaged (56%) in strong or very strong agreement. That question is the highest-scoring for the Disengaged, and nearly the highest for the Scripture Engaged. Many Bible readers see themselves as stewards of a planet that belongs to the Lord (Genesis 1:28–30; Psalm 24:1), but others have different reasons to feel strongly about the environment. On that and nearly every other pro-social issue, the Movable Middle seems comparatively unenthusiastic.

DEMOGRAPHICS

On all five issues, **women** are 10–18 percent more likely than men to agree strongly.[3]

While there are not wide differences among the **generations**, Gen Z is most likely to agree on the importance of caring for the environment; Millennials agree more than others on advocating for the oppressed; and those in the Boomer+ generation lead the way in befriending those of other races and religions.

On the importance of welcoming immigrants, people who live in the **West region** of the U.S. are 22 percent more likely to agree strongly than those in the Northeast, South, or Midwest.

---

3 Throughout this section, agreeing "strongly" also includes the "very strongly" response.

Across the board, greater levels of **education** mean greater agreement on the importance of all pro-social behaviors. On the importance of welcoming immigrants and advocating for the oppressed, those with at least some college education are more than 50 percent more likely to agree strongly than those with high school diplomas or less.

Those of **"Other Religions"** (non-Christian) are the most likely to agree strongly on the importance of four of the five pro-social behaviors. The **Nones** are most likely to agree strongly on caring for the environment, and they take a strong second on almost everything else. As for the four denominational groups, Mainline Protestants score high on the environment, Evangelicals on befriending those of other races and religions and advocating for the oppressed, and Catholics on welcoming immigrants.

GENEROSITY

"You are so rich in all you have: in faith, speech, and knowledge, in your eagerness to help and in your love for us. And so we want you to be generous also in this service of love" (2 Corinthians 8:7).

Generous giving has been part of the Christian experience from the beginning. It has always gone beyond amounts and percentages. Shortly after the challenge quoted above, the apostle reminds the Corinthians that "God loves a cheerful giver" (2 Corinthians 9:7 NIV). It has always been a matter of the heart.

With that in mind, we turn our attention to . . . amounts and percentages. Who gives what where? We value the widow's mite and the boy's five loaves, and we look for that spirit of generosity in the numbers. We trust that this information will help leaders plan wisely.

The Giving USA Foundation estimates that U.S. philanthropy totaled nearly $600 billion in 2024,[4] an increase of 6.3 percent over 2023 (or 3.3% when adjusted for inflation). After a couple of rough years, these figures are "consistent with long-term trends—clear evidence of Americans' enduring generosity and the value they place on non-profit work," according to Wendy McGrady, the Giving USA chair.

The news for the religious sector is not as rosy. While donations to religion grew 1.9 percent in current dollars, they actually decreased by 1 percent when adjusted for inflation.

Our numbers, based on reports from individual donors, generally jibe with the philanthropic data. There are slightly fewer givers than the previous year, but the median amount given has grown.

Basics of Charitable Giving, 2022–2024

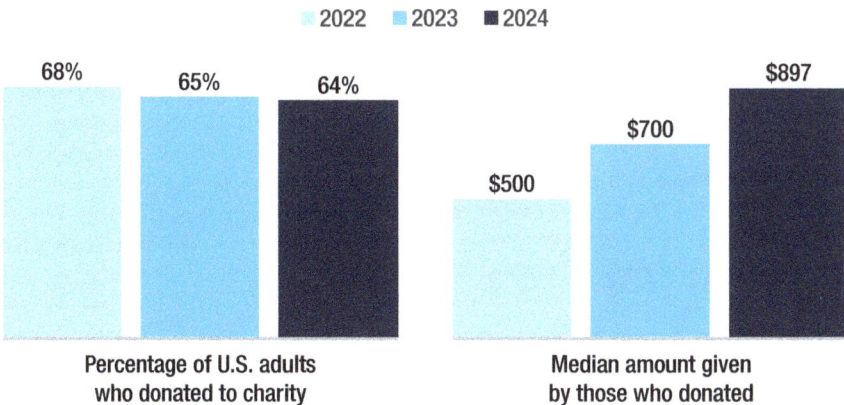

■ 2022   ■ 2023   ■ 2024

| 68% | 65% | 64% | | | $897 |

$700

$500

Percentage of U.S. adults
who donated to charity

Median amount given
by those who donated

---

4   $592.5 billion. Giving USA Foundation (2025). *Giving USA 2025: The Annual Report on Philanthropy for the Year 2024.* Available online at givingusa.org.

> "You are so rich in all you have: in faith, speech, and knowledge, in your eagerness to help and in your love for us. And so we want you to be generous also in this service of love."
>
> 2 Corinthians 8:7

About two-thirds of those responding to our survey report giving to churches, religious organizations, or other non-profit organizations, but this number has edged downward in the last two years, from 68 percent to 64 percent.

We prefer to compute the *median* amount given by these donors rather than the *mean,* which can be skewed by a few large gifts. The median finds the midpoint of donations made—essentially what the "average donor" gave. For 2024, exactly half of donors responding to our survey gave $897 or less, and exactly half gave that amount or more. This median represents an increase over the two previous years, suggesting that bigger donors donated more (perhaps buoyed by gains in the stock market?) while some smaller donors gave less (perhaps challenged by high inflation?).

Recipients of Donations

People give where they worship. Local churches, parishes, or temples receive the largest share of donations (40%) from individuals or households in our survey. Non-religious charities—either local (27%) or national (20%)—combine for nearly half of the donor dollar. Other religious organizations—either local (7%) or national (6%)—combine to receive about one eighth of charitable donations in the U.S.

Recipients of Donations, by Percentage Received

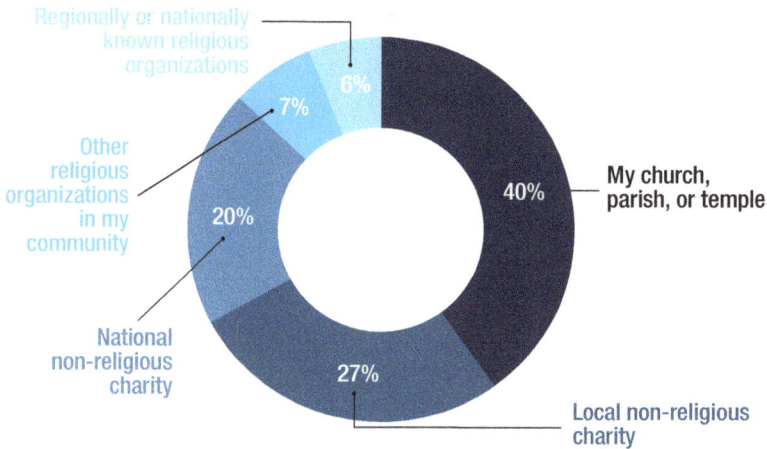

Regionally or nationally known religious organizations — 6%

Other religious organizations in my community — 7%

National non-religious charity — 20%

Local non-religious charity — 27%

My church, parish, or temple — 40%

GIVING AND SPIRITUAL FACTORS

Clearly, Scripture-engaged practicing Christians are not the only people who give to charity. That $592.5 billion came from a broad collection of individuals (as well as companies and foundations). But does a person's spiritual commitment affect their financial generosity? When people try to live out biblical teaching, does this extend to their money decisions? When people strongly agree that their faith is very important to them, do they back that up with charitable donations?

Scripture Engagement

We first look at Scripture engagement, finding a clear distinction among the three tiers. More than half of Bible Disengaged people

(51%) make some donation to charity, but that percentage rises sharply among the Movable Middle (75%) and even higher among the Scripture Engaged (86%).

There's also a huge difference in the median donation level, with the average Scripture Engaged donor ($2,000) giving four times the amount of the average Bible Disengaged donor ($500). Note that these median amounts do not take into account the zero figures of the non-donors. Of the donations made, these are the middle amounts.

It comes as no surprise that the majority of donations from the Scripture Engaged (66%) would support their local church. The remaining percentages, of course, go to other worthy charities, but the Scripture Engaged—and to a moderate level the Movable Middle (49%)—especially see the value of the local assembly.

Median Giving and Church Portion, by Scripture Engagement

■ % Giving Any Amount   ■ Median Charitable Giving   ■ Portion to Church/Parish/Temple

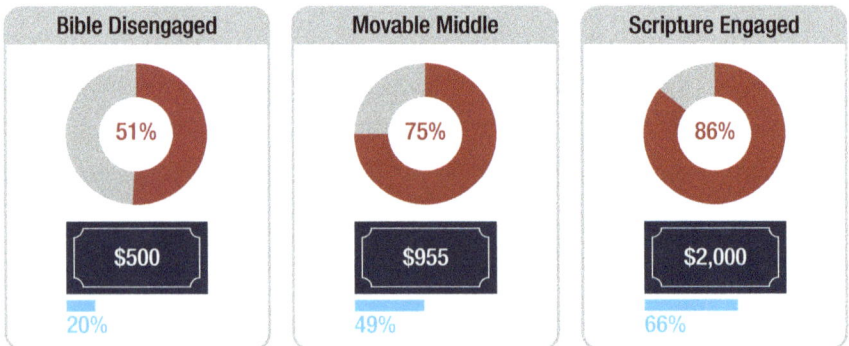

Bible Disengaged	Movable Middle	Scripture Engaged
51%	75%	86%
$500	$955	$2,000
20%	49%	66%

NOTE: Here, and throughout this section, we're taking the median amounts given by those who give. We're not including the zeroes from non-givers. These dollar figures reflect the midpoint of amounts given.

Faith Participation Levels

The four-tier Faith Participation metric shows some stark differences. **Nominal Christians**, who don't attend church even once a month, give far less to charity—any charity—than churchgoing Christians. As we would expect, the local church receives only a small portion (27%) of their charity dollar. **Casual Christians** attend church at least monthly, but differ from Practicing Christians on one point: they don't "strongly agree" that their faith is "very important" to them. How important could this one detail be? Well, here we see it in monetary terms (though there are a number of other spiritual ramifications as well). While nearly as many of them give to charity (87%), and they give three-fifths of their charity monies (60%) to the local church, the median amount they give is far short (half) of the Practicing Christians' level. By the way, the income levels of Practicing and Casual Christians are nearly identical, so this difference seems to come down to choices. Those who feel "strongly" that their faith is "very important," will express that faith in their financial decisions.

Median Giving and Church Portion, by Faith Participation Level

■ % Giving Any Amount ■ Median Charitable Giving ■ Portion to Church/Parish/Temple

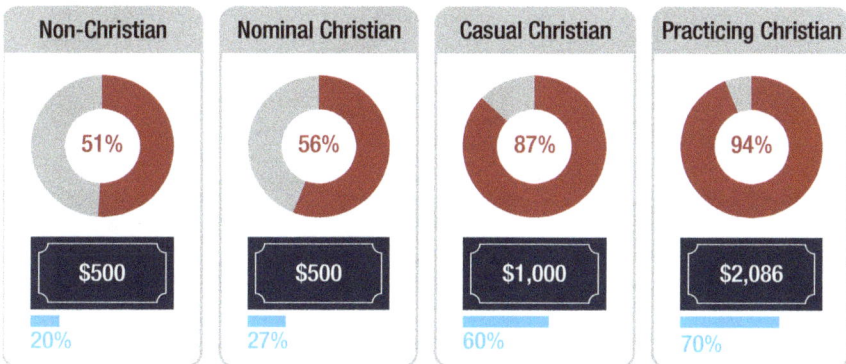

Non-Christian	Nominal Christian	Casual Christian	Practicing Christian
51%	56%	87%	94%
$500	$500	$1,000	$2,086
20%	27%	60%	70%

Denominations

As we turn our attention to giving patterns in different denominations, we find some significant differences.

Median Giving and Church Portion, by Denominational Group

■ % Giving Any Amount   ■ Median Charitable Giving   ■ Portion to Church/Parish/Temple

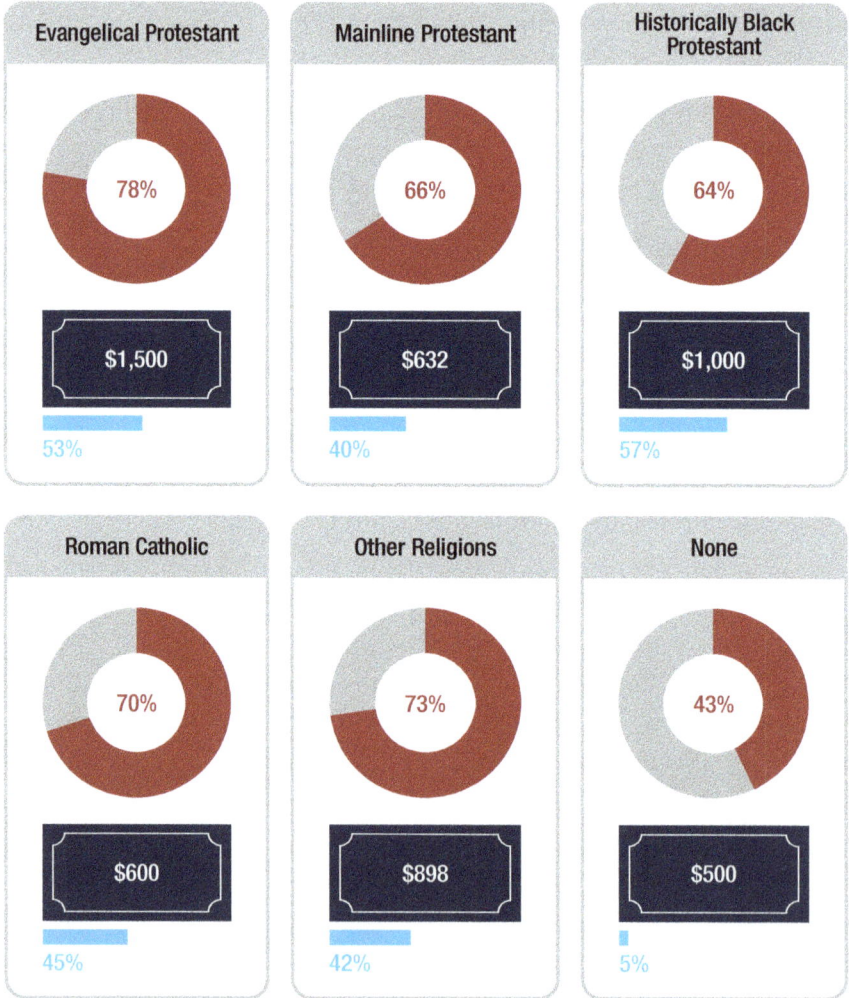

Evangelical Protestant

78%

$1,500

53%

Mainline Protestant

66%

$632

40%

Historically Black Protestant

64%

$1,000

57%

Roman Catholic

70%

$600

45%

Other Religions

73%

$898

42%

None

43%

$500

5%

Evangelical Protestants have the highest percentage of givers (78%) and, by far, the highest median amount given ($1,500). Among other religious groups—including non-Christian religions—the percentage of givers is 5–14 points lower. **Historically Black Protestant** churches have a relatively high median amount given ($1,000) and the highest percentage going to the local church. **Mainline Protestants** give the lowest percentage (40%) to the local church.

How People Attend Church

How does the mode of church attendance—in-person or online—correspond with people's charitable giving? More than nine in ten (92%) of those who attend church primarily in person donate *something* to charity. That percentage is nearly the same (89%) for those who split their churchgoing between the two modes. But only about three in five of those who attend church primarily online (60%) are donors. For churches that use their online ministry as a "front porch," drawing new people in with low-risk connections, this is not surprising.

Percent Who Give and Median Amount, by How People Attend

■ Donors   ■ Median Amount Given by Donors

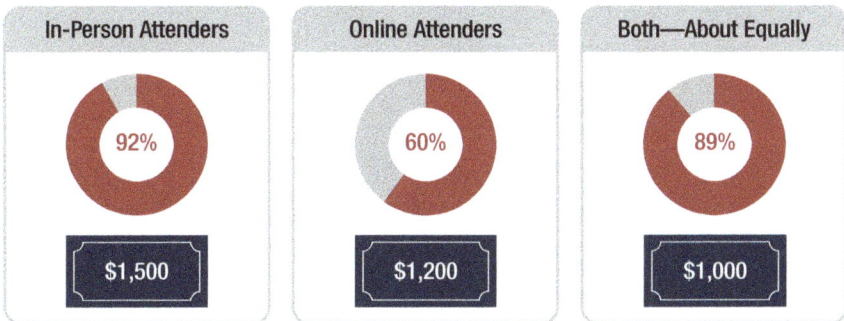

In-Person Attenders	Online Attenders	Both—About Equally
92%	60%	89%
$1,500	$1,200	$1,000

Also unsurprising: In-person attenders give the most money to charity. (Note that this reflects all charitable giving, not just to the church.) This may reflect a number of cultural factors, including generation and income level—which may be different among those most comfortable with online attendance—but it might also demonstrate varying levels of commitment to the church.

WHERE YOUR TREASURE IS

Jesus said, "Where your treasure is, there your heart will be also" (Matthew 6:21 NIV). In fact, he taught about money a lot. Not that he was raising funds for some new ministry project, but he understood the connection between passion and possessions. Riches can lure people into ruin. Money makes a bad master.

Loving Behavior by Frequency of Bible Use

"As a result of using the Bible, within the past month, I show more loving behavior towards others."

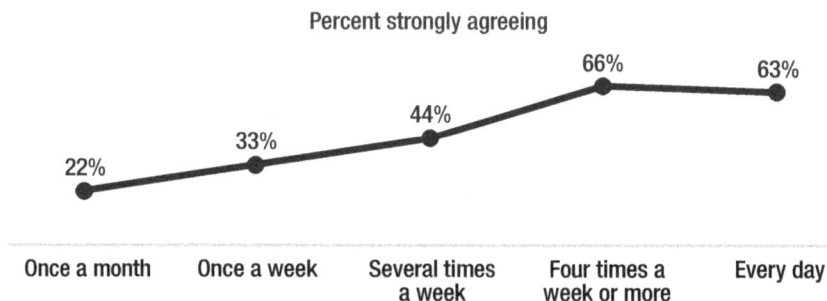

Percent strongly agreeing

Once a month	Once a week	Several times a week	Four times a week or more	Every day
22%	33%	44%	66%	63%

But people who are motivated by the love of Christ find freedom in giving money away for good purposes—helping people, doing God's work in the world. Financial donation is but one form of the generosity that floods the hearts of the faithful.

Generosity by Frequency of Bible Use

*"As a result of using the Bible, within the past month,
I am more generous with my time, energy, or financial resources."*

Percent strongly agreeing

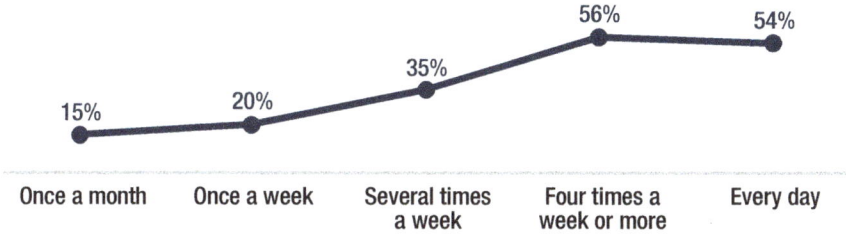

Once a month	Once a week	Several times a week	Four times a week or more	Every day
15%	20%	35%	56%	54%

We end this chapter where we began: *As a result of using the Bible*, are people more loving in their behavior and more generous with their time, energy and money? Does Scripture make a difference?

Clearly it does. On both questions—loving behavior and generosity—those who read the Bible most frequently are far more likely to agree strongly about its impact in their lives. As we regularly interact with God in Scripture, we are changed for the better. ▪

LOVE IN ACTION

In this episode, we interview **Heath Adamson**, author, speaker, advocate, and Senior Vice President of Global Programs at Convoy of Hope, one of the 50 largest charities in the United States. Tune in to hear how the message of the Bible has mobilized Heath and his ministry to love and serve neighbors far and wide.

State of the Bible
THE PODCAST

AMERICAN BIBLE SOCIETY

The Impact of Scripture Engagement

on Loving Behaviors

Pro-Social Attitudes by Scripture Engagement, 2025

Percent who "strongly" or "very strongly" agree

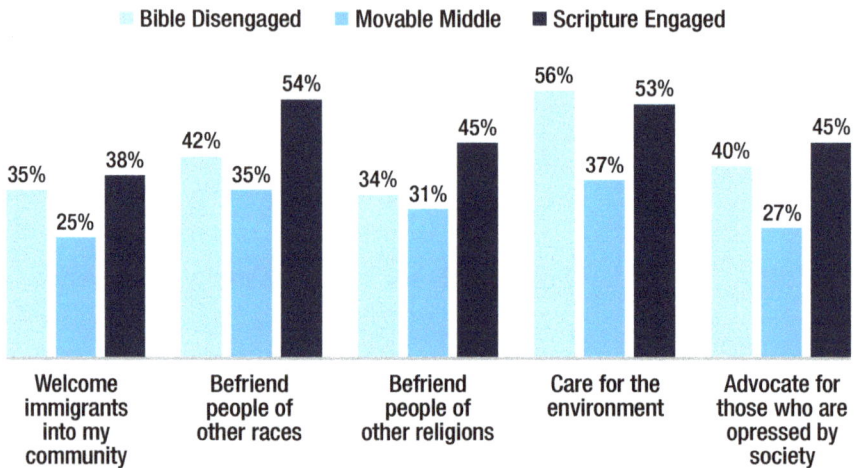

- Bible Disengaged
- Movable Middle
- Scripture Engaged

	Welcome immigrants into my community	Befriend people of other races	Befriend people of other religions	Care for the environment	Advocate for those who are opressed by society
Bible Disengaged	35%	42%	34%	56%	40%
Movable Middle	25%	35%	31%	37%	27%
Scripture Engaged	38%	54%	45%	53%	45%

on Generosity

Median Giving and Church Portion, by Scripture Engagement

- % Giving Any Amount
- Median Charitable Giving
- Portion to Church/Parish/Temple

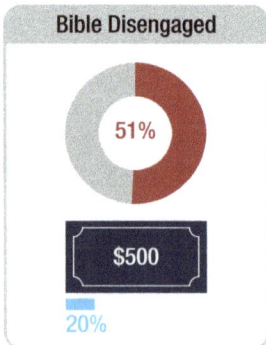

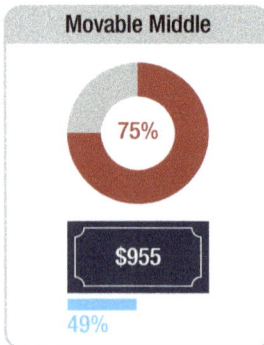

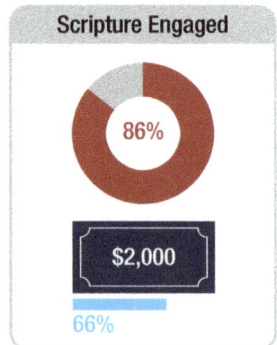

Bible Disengaged
51%
$500
20%

Movable Middle
75%
$955
49%

Scripture Engaged
86%
$2,000
66%

CHAPTER 9

LOOKING BACK AND LOOKING FORWARD

Reliable information propels good leadership. This applies not only to corporate CEOs, but to anyone seeking to make a difference. We need to know how things are, how things are changing, and how people feel about that.

State of the Bible 2025 has gathered a great deal of information about society and the church. We have explored the attitudes and actions of the general public and particularly Christians. We have tried to provide you with lenses to help you view your work in the world, whether you're a pastor, a ministry leader, or a Christian trying to "speak the truth in love" to your neighbor.

As we conclude this year's report, what can we identify as the major stories, the happy surprises, the emerging needs? We humbly offer our top ten, in no particular order.

1

After three down years, Scripture Engagement and Bible Use are up

Millennials and men fuel much of that increase

For the first time in four years, we saw an increase in the percentage of Americans who are Scripture Engaged (20%, up from 18%). There was a corresponding rise in Bible Users (41%, up from 38%).

Most of the increase in Bible Use came from Millennials, who saw a 9-point rise (39%, up from 30%). That generation also climbed 5 points (from 12% to 17%) in Scripture Engagement. In every generation, men increased in Bible Use over last year (34% to 41% overall).

This is encouraging news after a precipitous decline earlier this decade. Scripture Engagement had dropped 10 points (28% to 18%) between 2020 and 2023 (see Chapter 1 for details).

Maybe we're beginning a climb back up to those previous levels. One year doesn't make a trend, but we do sense stirrings of renewed interest in Scripture throughout our culture.

2

The U.S. leads the Secular West in Bible Use

Americans more likely to see its relevance and want to learn more

We were honored to be part of the Patmos Initiative, an international survey sponsored by our colleagues in the United Bible Societies (see Chapter 2 for details). Seven different "clusters" of nations were identified and polled about Bible-related attitudes and actions. The U.S. took its place in the group called the Secular West, including much of Europe and other English-speaking nations. We compared findings from the U.S. with those of other countries in this cluster.

It was encouraging to see Americans at or near the top in our relationship with the Bible, but discouraging to see the low scores from other nations—especially as we recognize the rich history of Christianity in those same countries.

While about two in five Americans say they use the Bible at least monthly, the next closest countries (Italy and Ireland) show only 28 percent at that level.

More than half (51%) of Americans say, "The Bible is relevant to me personally." No other nation in the cluster tops 40 percent, and the median is 25 percent.

More than a third of Americans (34%) say they're "very interested" in learning more about the Bible. Second place goes to Ireland at only 19 percent.

What we asked toward the end of that chapter bears repeating. "Are the statistics from the rest of the Secular West a glimpse of America's future or a cautionary tale of decline that can be avoided? Also, how can American Christians advocate for the Bible at home and around the world, particularly helping others in our cluster of nations to re-engage with Scripture?"

SUBSCRIBE TO OUR PODCAST

Join us as we unpack the latest data on Bible use and Scripture engagement and their impact on faith, trust, church engagement, and well-being. You'll hear from thought leaders who provide deeper insights beyond the numbers. Subscribe to the *State of the Bible* podcast for the latest.

State of the Bible
THE PODCAST

AMERICAN BIBLE SOCIETY

3

Americans flourishing again after COVID plunge

Numbers surpass pre-pandemic levels

In 2020, we began using the Human Flourishing Index (see Chapter 3) just in time to develop a pre-pandemic baseline and then chart the downs and ups of America's struggle with COVID. It took a couple of years to get back to where we had been, but now in every category Americans score even higher than pre-COVID levels—with one exception: Mental & Physical Health, which has fought its way up to the same level where it was in January 2020 (see graph on page 51).

2-MINUTE INSIGHTS

Two minutes is all you need to catch the highlights. Scroll through our short Insights videos to better understand what people think about and how they interact with the Bible.

4

Flourishing increases with frequency of Bible Use

Bible Study Groups also prove helpful

News flash: Bible reading is good for you.

We knew that, of course, but here's documentation, thanks to the Human Flourishing Index, a metric developed by Harvard researchers. People who never read the Bible have a rather low flourishing score (6.8). Those who interact with Scripture three or four times a year have a slightly higher score (7.1). But the score shoots up quickly for those who use the Bible at least four times a week (7.8) or every day (7.9).

If you're trying to help people start a Bible reading habit, this is rather convincing evidence that it can improve their lives in many ways (see graph on page 60).

Being in a Bible study group is another way to have a better life. Group members had an average Human Flourishing score of 7.9, far exceeding the national average in every domain.

5

Two-thirds of Bible Users access it digitally

Bible Engagement is now fully multimedia

How many pastors have begun to say, "Turn to today's Scripture in your Bibles *or on your phone*"? Bible use is changing as new technology becomes more accessible to more people.

Among Bible Users in America, two of three (66%) use digital devices for their Bible use, at least sometimes. As you'd expect, younger Bible Users are more likely to use digital formats than Boomers and Elders (three quarters of Gen X, Gen Z, and Millennial Bible Users). Gen Z is much more likely than any other age group to interact with Scripture in video form.

Digital formats can make Bible study easier, but will they enable people to interact with Scripture in a deeper, more committed way? That will be a continuing challenge for those in ministry.

6

Church Engagement improves well-being

Stress, loneliness drop with greater church connections

We introduced a new metric this year: Church Engagement, based on five simple questions about people's spiritual and social interactions at church (see Chapter 5 for details).

It only makes sense that Church Engagement starts with attendance. Those who attend weekly report far more engagement than those who attend monthly. *In-person* attendance is also connected with greater Church Engagement, compared to online attendance or a mixture of both. But there's more to Church Engagement than just being there. The CE questions ask about opportunities to grow spiritually and to use spiritual gifts. Also, among those with high Church Engagement, about five of six agree that "the message of the Bible has transformed my life" (more than doubling the portion of those with average CE).

We also found that Generation Z scored lowest in Church Engagement on all five questions, suggesting that church leaders may need to do more to include and equip their youngest attenders.

One of the most interesting findings on Church Engagement came when we cross-tabulated it with Well-Being—a collection of personal issues—stress, anxiety, loneliness, hope—we've measured for several years now. When people engage with a church, do they enjoy greater Well-Being?

Yes, the statistics are clear. People with high Church Engagement scores have significantly less stress, less anxiety, less loneliness, and more hope (see graph on page 103).

CHURCH LEADERS TOOLKIT

Want to share these insights with others? Now you can! All of the *State of the Bible 2025* visualizations are now available for download on the Resources page of our new website!

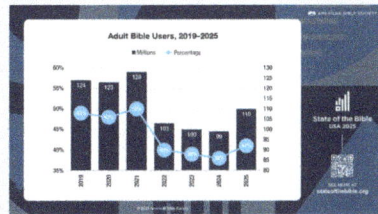

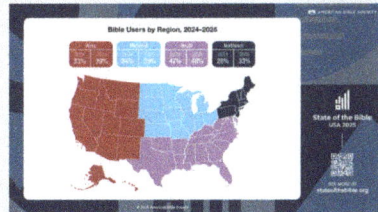

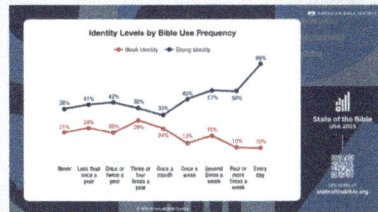

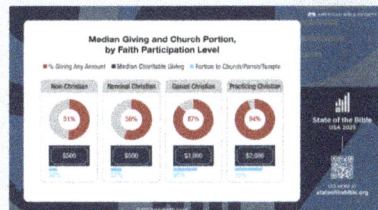

7

Gen Z men have weakest sense of identity

Far outpaced by Gen Z women

Another new metric this year is an Identity score, based on three core questions derived from psychological studies. Answers yielded a level of Strong, Moderate, or Weak Identity (see Chapter 6 for details).

Identity tends to strengthen with age. Each older generation has more in the Strong Identity group and fewer with Weak Identity. Women also show stronger identity than men in every generation.

Notably, Gen Z men display something of an identity crisis, with the fewest Strong and the most Weak. On the other hand, Gen Z women break the trend by outscoring their older Millennial sisters in Strong Identity.

We also found that a weak sense of Identity is associated with greater stress, anxiety, and loneliness. Is this something these young men will grow out of? Perhaps. But church leaders should be aware and provide appropriate care.

8 Practice of faith linked to stronger identity

Casuals, Nominals, Nones fall short of Practicing Christians

Practicing Christians, in our surveys, are self-identified Christians who attend church (in some form) at least once a month and consider their faith very important in their lives. Last year we began isolating two Non-Practicing groups: Nominal Christians, who don't attend monthly; and Casual Christians, who attend monthly but don't consider their faith very important.

Nearly two-thirds (64%) of Practicing Christians have a strong Identity score, based on our three questions. This is far more than Casuals (33%), Nominals (40%), or Nones (33%).

This suggests the benefit of not only claiming faith, but practicing it, and identifying it as an "important" part of one's life.

9

Multi-year slide in pro-social attitudes 2022–25

Movable Middle scores lowest

For years now, we've asked about "pro-social" attitudes. Do people feel it's important to . . . welcome immigrants, befriend people of other races or religions, care for the environment, or advocate for the oppressed? For this report, we also looked back at results from three previous years. The results were telling (see chart on page 157).

Between 2022 and 2025, there was a gradual downward slide in the percentage of those agreeing "strongly" or "very strongly" on the importance of these issues.

As we filtered the current year's findings by Scripture engagement, we found another interesting development. The Scripture Engaged and Bible Disengaged are rather close in their levels of agreement, with the Movable Middle trailing behind on every issue (see chart on page 158).

10

Three times as many trust the Bible as are skeptical

'Nones' remain deeply suspicious

Nearly one in five Americans (18%, and half of the religious "nones") believe the Bible was written "to control or manipulate people." It's a shame there are so many. Perhaps we can engage some of them in loving conversations that change their minds.

But twice as many (36%) believe that "the Bible is totally accurate in all the principles it presents." Trust in the Bible is still very much alive.

And beyond what people believe *about* Scripture, there's the question of how they connect with it. Do they meet God there? Apparently many more do. Well more than half of Americans (58%) are willing to say, "The message of the Bible has transformed my life."

SCRIPTURE ENGAGEMENT:
SEVEN CONNECTIONS

We take every opportunity to promote Scripture Engagement—not just reading the Bible regularly, but living it out. As people encounter God in the Bible, we can see measurable positive effects. Here's a quick review of seven connections.

1 · **7.9** ⬆

The Scripture Engaged score higher on the **Human Flourishing Index** with an overall score of 7.9 (Movable Middle has 7.0 and Bible Disengaged 6.8). The aspect of flourishing with the greatest difference is Meaning & Purpose. *See pages 61–62.*

2 · **HOPE** ⬆

On topics related to **Well-Being**, we found that regular Bible reading is linked to lower levels of stress, anxiety, and loneliness, and higher levels of hope. *See page 83.*

3 · ● ● ● ● ● ●

Five out of six of the Scripture Engaged (83%) strongly agree with the statement *"I consider my faith to be a great source of comfort when I am struggling with life issues"* (Movable Middle, only 37%). *See page 86.*

4 · **4X**

More than half of the Scripture Engaged (52%) also have high **Church Engagement**, four times the level of the Movable Middle (13%). *See page 104.*

5

Nearly two-thirds of Scripture Engaged people (63%) exhibit a strong sense of **Identity**, far more than the Movable Middle or Bible Disengaged (both 38%). *See page 121.*

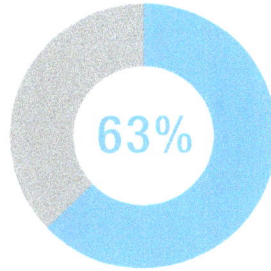

6

More than a third of the Scripture Engaged score at the high level of **Interpersonal Trust** (compared to 24 percent for the Movable Middle). *See page 137.*

7

Nearly nine in ten of the Scripture Engaged (86%) **give to charity**, compared to 75 percent of the Movable Middle. Scripture engaged donors also give twice as much on average, and they give a greater portion to the church (66%, compared to the MM's 49%). *See page 164.*

66%

2026 LINEUP

Only God knows what the next year will bring. But we're already planning the questions to include on our 2026 survey. We will continue to update you on the basics of our society's interaction with Scripture, and we hope to explore some new issues as well. Here are some of the chapters we expect to include next year.

The Bible in America. Our annual scorecard on Scripture Engagement, Bible Use, and other key indicators. What parts of the Bible do people read most? Where do they turn when they don't understand?

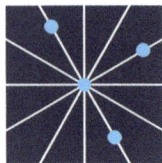

Supernatural Beliefs and Practices. What do Americans believe about resurrection, about angels and demons, about heaven and hell, about miracles and temptations, about alternate spiritualities and magical practices? How do Christians apply biblical teaching to these matters?

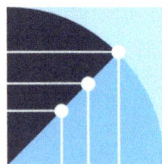

Parenting and the Bible. How do parents bring up their children "in the way they should go"? How are children learning the Bible, faith, and Christian behavior? Do parents feel supported by their churches? What seems to be working and what isn't? Can we identify "best practices" in this crucial task?

Artificial Intelligence. Tool or tyrant? Ministry blessing or Mark of the Beast? How is it being used, and how do people feel about it—in the church and in society? Does it enhance preaching or Bible education or church fellowship, or is it a new "graven image"?

Church Health. Exploring the factors exhibited by healthy churches and vibrant congregations. We'll build on this year's Church Engagement data to see how churches in America are doing, and perhaps we'll get some ideas on how they can operate more effectively.

Forgiveness. Easy to preach about, hard to do. It's a pivotal part of the prayer Jesus taught his disciples. Where do we encounter it in today's world? How do people practice and receive forgiveness, and what difference does it make in their lives?

Love and Flourishing. Our Harvard friends are adding a new element to their study of Human Flourishing—love—noting its importance in our relationships and communities, as well as our personal psychology. Of course, we at *State of the Bible* are well aware of biblical teaching on the subject, and we're eager to continue partnering with them in this new exploration.

We hope that *State of the Bible 2025* has been informative and, well, *engaging*. We look forward to serving you again in 2026.

METHODOLOGY

I n 2025, the *State of the Bible* research team at American Bible Society collaborated with NORC at the University of Chicago to design and field a nationally representative survey of American adults on topics related to the Bible, faith, and the church. The study was conducted in English and was presented both online and via telephone to NORC's AmeriSpeak® Panel, using a 19-minute questionnaire. The study produced 2,656 responses from a representative sample of adults 18 and older within all 50 states and the District of Columbia. Data were collected from January 2–21, 2025. The margin of error for a sample of this size is ±2.47 percent at the 95 percent confidence level.

QUALITY AT A GLANCE

Following are key survey quality indicators, excerpted from a report card prepared by NORC at the University of Chicago in compliance with the American Association for Public Opinion Research

(AAPOR) Transparency Initiative. The full report is available upon request by emailing pr@americanbible.org.

SURVEY OVERVIEW

- **Study Population:** General Population Age 18+
- **Sample Units:** 13,156
- **Completed Units:** 2,656
- **Margin of Error:** ±2.47%
- **Average Design Effect:** 1.69
- **Survey Field Period:** January 2–21, 2025
- **Median Duration:** 19 minutes

PANEL OUTCOMES

- **Weighted Household Recruitment Rate:**[1] 27.4%
- **Weighted Household Retention Rate:** 77.2%

SURVEY OUTCOMES

- **Survey Completion Rate:**[2] 20.2%
- **Weighted Cumulative Response Rate:**[3] 4.3%

---

1   The weighted AAPOR RR III for the AmeriSpeak panel recruitment corresponding to the recruitment cohorts sampled for the study. A recruited household is a household where at least one adult successfully completed the recruitment survey and joined the panel.
2   The percent of eligible sample members who completed the survey interview.
3   The overall survey response rate that accounts for survey outcomes in all response stages including panel recruitment rate, panel retention rate, and survey completion rate. It is weighted to account for the sample design and differential inclusion probabilities of sample members.

THE AMERISPEAK® PANEL

Funded and operated by NORC at the University of Chicago, AmeriSpeak® is a probability-based panel designed to be representative of the U.S. household population. Randomly selected U.S. households are sampled using area probability and address-based sampling, with a known, non-zero probability of selection from the NORC National Sample Frame. These sampled households are then contacted by U.S. mail, telephone, and field interviewers (face to face).

The panel provides sample coverage of approximately 97 percent of the U.S. household population. Those excluded from the sample include people with PO Box addresses, some addresses not listed in the USPS Delivery Sequence File, and some newly constructed dwellings.

While most AmeriSpeak households participate in surveys by web, non-internet households can participate in AmeriSpeak surveys by telephone. Households without conventional internet access but having web access via smartphones are allowed to participate in AmeriSpeak surveys by web. AmeriSpeak panelists participate in NORC studies or studies conducted by NORC on behalf of governmental agencies, academic researchers, and media and commercial organizations.

For more information, email AmeriSpeak-BD@norc.org or visit AmeriSpeak.norc.org.

NORC at the University of Chicago is an independent research institution that delivers reliable data and rigorous analysis to guide critical programmatic, business, and policy decisions. Since 1941,

NORC has conducted groundbreaking studies, created and applied innovative methods and tools, and advanced principles of scientific integrity and collaboration. Today, government, corporate, and nonprofit clients around the world partner with NORC to transform increasingly complex information into useful knowledge. Please visit www.norc.org for more information. ◼

DEFINITIONS

T he following definitions are used in this and other *State of the Bible* reports to group respondents by demographics, beliefs, and practices.

Bible Skeptic: Individuals who believe the Bible is just another book written by people that contains stories and advice.

Bible User: Individuals who read, listen to, or pray with the Bible on their own at least 3–4 times a year, outside of a church service or church event.

Church Engagement: We measure the level of commitment and connection a person might experience in their church using five items inspired by the Gallup Q12® questions for employee engagement.[1]

1. At church. I have the opportunity to use my giftings.
2. My pastor, or other church leaders, seem to care about me as a person.
3. There is someone in my church who encourages my spiritual development.

---

1 Buckingham, M., & Harter, J. (1999). *First, Break All the Rules: What the World's Greatest Managers Do Differently.* Gallup Press.

4. I have a best friend at church.
5. In the past year I have had opportunities to learn and grow in my faith.

Churched: Individuals who have attended a Christian church service in the past six months for any reason other than a special occasion, such as a wedding or funeral.

Consolidated Identity: The extent to which an individual has developed a coherent, grounded, and positive sense of self. We measure it using three items from the Consolidated Identity scale of the Self-Concept and Identity Measure.[2]

1. I know who I am.
2. I always have a good sense about what is important to me.
3. I know what I believe or value.

Correlation: In statistics, the strength of a linear relationship between two variables is often expressed as a numerical value preceded by the italicized letter r. We report correlations only when they are statistically significant ($p < .05$) and when the correlation coefficient (r) is 0.2 or greater. We use these rules of thumb for interpreting the qualitative magnitude of a correlation:

- Very Weak ($r = 0.00—0.19$)
- Weak ($r = 0.20—0.39$)
- Moderate ($r = 0.40—0.59$)
- Strong ($r = 0.60—0.79$)
- Very Strong ($r = 0.80—1.00$)

---

2 Kaufman, E. A., Puzia, M. E., Crowell, S. E., & Price, C. J. (2019). Replication of the Self-Concept and Identity Measure (SCIM) Among a Treatment-Seeking Sample. *Identity, 19* (1), 18–28. https://doi.org/10.1080/15283488.2019.1566068

Division: The U.S. Census Bureau divides the United States into nine geographic divisions, which are groupings of multiple states. These divisions and their population characteristics are used to ensure that survey responses are demographically representative of the United States as a whole.

Generations:

- **Generation Z (1997–2012):** Ages 13 to 28 in 2025. This study includes adults (18–28) in Generation Z.
- **Millennials (1981–1996):** Ages 29 to 44 in 2025.
- **Generation X (1965–1980):** Ages 45 to 60 in 2025.
- **Baby Boomers (1946–1964):** Ages 61 to 79 in 2025.
- **Elders (1928–1945):** This study places considers any respondent 80 years old or older to be in the Elders generation. Due to sampling limitations for people of this age, this small group is combined with the Baby Boomer group and listed in the report as **Boomers+.**

Hope Agency: This is a measure of an individual's perceived capacity for initiating and maintaining the actions necessary to reach a goal. It is measured with three items. Scores range from 3–24.[3]

1. At the present, I am energetically pursuing my life plan.
2. Right now, I can see myself as being pretty successful in navigating life.
3. At this time, I am meeting the life goals that I have set for myself.

---

3 Snyder, C. R., Harris, C., Anderson, J. R., Holleran, S. A., Irving, L. M., Sigmon, S. T, Yoshinobu, L., Gibb, J., Langelle, C., & Hamey, P. (1991). The will and the ways: Development and validation of an individual-differences measure of hope. *Journal of Personality and Social Psychology, 60,* 570–585.

Human Flourishing Index: While healthcare often focuses on pathology—what's wrong—this is an effort to see health in a positive way. The Human Flourishing Index emerged at Harvard University's T. H. Chan School of Public Health in 2017.[4] It has been used (with permission) in the *State of the Bible* since 2020. Researchers focus on six areas of the human experience ("domains"), asking two questions about each.

1. Happiness & Life Satisfaction
2. Mental & Physical Health
3. Meaning & Purpose
4. Character & Virtue
5. Close Social Relationships
6. Financial & Material Stability

The results yield two composite scores on a 0 to 10 scale: the *Human Flourishing Index* (which leaves out the financial domain) and the *Secure Flourishing Index* (which includes it).

Loneliness: We measure loneliness using five items from the UCLA Loneliness Scale.[5]

- How often do you feel alone?
- How often do you feel that you are no longer close to anyone?
- How often do you feel left out?
- How often do you feel that no one really knows you well?
- How often do you feel that people are around you but not with you?

---

4 VanderWeele, T. J. (2017). On the promotion of human flourishing. *Proceedings of the National Academy of Sciences, 114*(31), 8148–56.

5 Russell, D. (1996). UCLA Loneliness Scale (Version 3): Reliability, validity, and factor structure. *Journal of Personality Assessment, 66,* 20–40.

Loneliness scores range from 5–20. We have grouped them into three levels.

- Low: 5–9
- Moderate: 10–15
- High: 16–20

No faith/Other faith: Individuals who do not consider themselves Christian (including atheists, agnostics, and other faiths). Mormons and Jehovah's Witnesses are also included, even if they describe themselves as Christian.

Non-Christian: Individuals who consider themselves to be anything other than Christians. This includes those of other faiths (see above) as well as the **Nones,** who do not identify with any religion at all.

Non-Practicing Christian: Self-identified Christians who are not Practicing Christians as defined below. Two subsets of this group are **Nominals,** who identify as Christians but do not attend church at least monthly, and **Casuals,** who identify and attend but do not "strongly agree" that their faith is very important in their lives.

Practicing Christian: Individuals who meet all three of the following criteria:

- Self-identify as Christian, adhering to a historically biblical tradition
- Attend a religious service at least once a month
- Say their faith is very important in their lives

Pathway of Scripture Engagement: American Bible Society's theory of change: a ten-step logic model describing how individuals with access to the Bible receive it, interact with it, and ultimately are changed by it. See *Appendix 3: Pathway of Scripture Engagement* for further detail.

Region: The U.S. Census Bureau divides the United States into four geographic regions, which are groupings of multiple divisions. These regions and their population characteristics are used to ensure that survey responses are demographically representative of the United States as a whole.

Scripture engaged: Anyone who scores 100 or higher on the Scripture Engagement Scale.

Scripture unengaged: Anyone who scores below 100 on the Scripture Engagement Scale.

Scripture Engagement Scale: Based on responses to 14 survey items about the frequency of Bible use and the impact and centrality of its message, this scale provides a high-fidelity, numerical measure of holistic Scripture engagement among U.S. Bible Users. The Scripture Engagement Scale is centered on 100, meaning that approximately one half of U.S. Bible Users score above 100, and the other half score below 100. The scale's standard deviation is 15.

Scripture Engagement Segments (Full): The Scripture engagement of individuals and groups can be described using the following five segments based on Scripture Engagement Scale scores.

1. **Bible Centered**   Score = 115 or higher.
2. **Bible Engaged**   Score = 100–114.
3. **Bible Friendly**   Score = 85–99.
4. **Bible Neutral**   Score = 70–84.
5. **Bible Disengaged**   Score = Less than 70.

Scripture Engagement Segments (Simplified): The Scripture engagement of individuals and groups can also be described using the following three segments based on Scripture Engagement Scale scores.

1. **Scripture Engaged:** Score = 100 or higher. Includes both the Bible Centered and the Bible Engaged.
2. **Movable Middle:** Score = 70–99. Includes both the Bible Friendly and Bible Neutral categories.
3. **Bible Disengaged:** Score = Less than 70. Same as Bible Disengaged in the Full Scripture Engagement segmentation.

Self-Identified Religion: Respondents are asked, "do you consider yourself any of the following religious faiths?" Their response is their self-identified religion, regardless of their current involvement with any religious organization.

Spiritual Vitality Gauge (SVG): From answers to nine concise questions focusing on beliefs, spiritual practices, and faith in action, the SVG yields a score between 0 and 100 as a reliable measure of spiritual health. The questions are asked only of self-identifying Christians. The SVG is used by permission of Renovo.

Spiritual Vitality Segments: We place self-identifying Christian respondents into one of four descriptive groups based on their SVG scores:

1. **Ailing**   Score = 0–50
2. **Unhealthy**   Score = 51–70
3. **Healthy**   Score = 71–90
4. **Thriving**   Score = 91–100

Trauma Impact: Respondents who have experienced at least one traumatic event are asked, "Does the trauma you experienced or witnessed still affect you today? *Select one.*" Response options are:

- Always
- Most of the time
- About half the time
- Sometimes
- Never

Trauma Incidence: Respondents are asked, "Have you ever experienced or witnessed physical, psychological, or emotional trauma? That is, extreme violence, abuse, or a near-death experience that produces a response of intense fear, helplessness, or horror? *Check all that apply.*" Response options are:

- You personally experienced a trauma
- You witnessed a trauma
- None of these apply to me

Respondents who select *any option except* "none of these apply to me" are counted as having experienced trauma.

Trauma Severity: Respondents who experience the impact of trauma at least "sometimes" are asked, "Please rate the **severity** of the trauma effects you are experiencing on the scale below." The numerical response scale has a range of 1–10 with the following qualitative anchors:

- 0 = None
- 5 = Moderate
- 10 = Overwhelming

Trust: We measure interpersonal trust using five items from the General Trust Scale.[6]

1. Most people are basically honest.
2. Most people are trustworthy.
3. I am trusting of others.
4. Most people are sincere and well-intentioned.
5. People will usually keep their promises if they make them.

Unchurched: Individuals who have not attended a Christian church service in the past six months for any reason other than a special occasion, such as a wedding or funeral.

---

6 Yamagishi, T. & Yamagishi, M. (1994). Trust and commitment in the United States and Japan. *Motivation and Emotion, 18* (2), 129–166.

PATHWAY OF SCRIPTURE ENGAGEMENT

The Pathway of Scripture Engagement (PSE) is American Bible Society's theory of change: a ten-step logic model describing how individuals with access to the Bible receive it, interact with it, and ultimately are changed by it. The PSE is the foundation of our empirical research, which shows that consistent interaction with the Bible shapes people's choices and transforms their relationships with God, self, and others.

PURPOSE OF THE PATHWAY

The PSE marks out a set of waypoints along a journey of spiritual formation. When the Bible is made available through translation and distribution, pilgrims may enter the Pathway and begin their journey toward reconciliation with God and others.

The journey along the Pathway brings its own benefits, including wisdom for daily living, increased awareness of God's presence and voice, and generosity of spirit and action. However, what makes the Pathway uniquely valuable is its destination: spiritual health and vitality marked by deeply rooted love for God and healthy relationships with others, particularly those in the community of faith.

The PSE is like a ladder with ten rungs. Users might climb one rung at a time or even skip a rung. They may climb slowly or quickly. It's even possible to climb part of the way up the ladder and then retreat a few steps. As users climb the ladder, their perspective changes with altitude and as distant objects draw nearer. Still, the most important thing about a ladder is that it's leaning against the right building. Similarly, the most important thing about Scripture Engagement is that it is leaning against the building of holistic spiritual vitality marked by love for God and others. According to Jesus, loving God and others are the two great commandments for all his followers (Matthew 22:37–39).

PROGRESS ALONG THE PATHWAY

The Pathway of Scripture Engagement is also like an old-school map that marks out a journey from beginning to end. The PSE is for anyone who has access to the Bible in their own language because the Bible is the primary vehicle that carries people toward spiritual health.

The PSE shows the landscape and key waypoints, but it doesn't do two important things. First, it doesn't have a YOU ARE HERE marker. Second, it doesn't measure progress toward spiritual vitality. For

The Pathway of Scripture Engagement

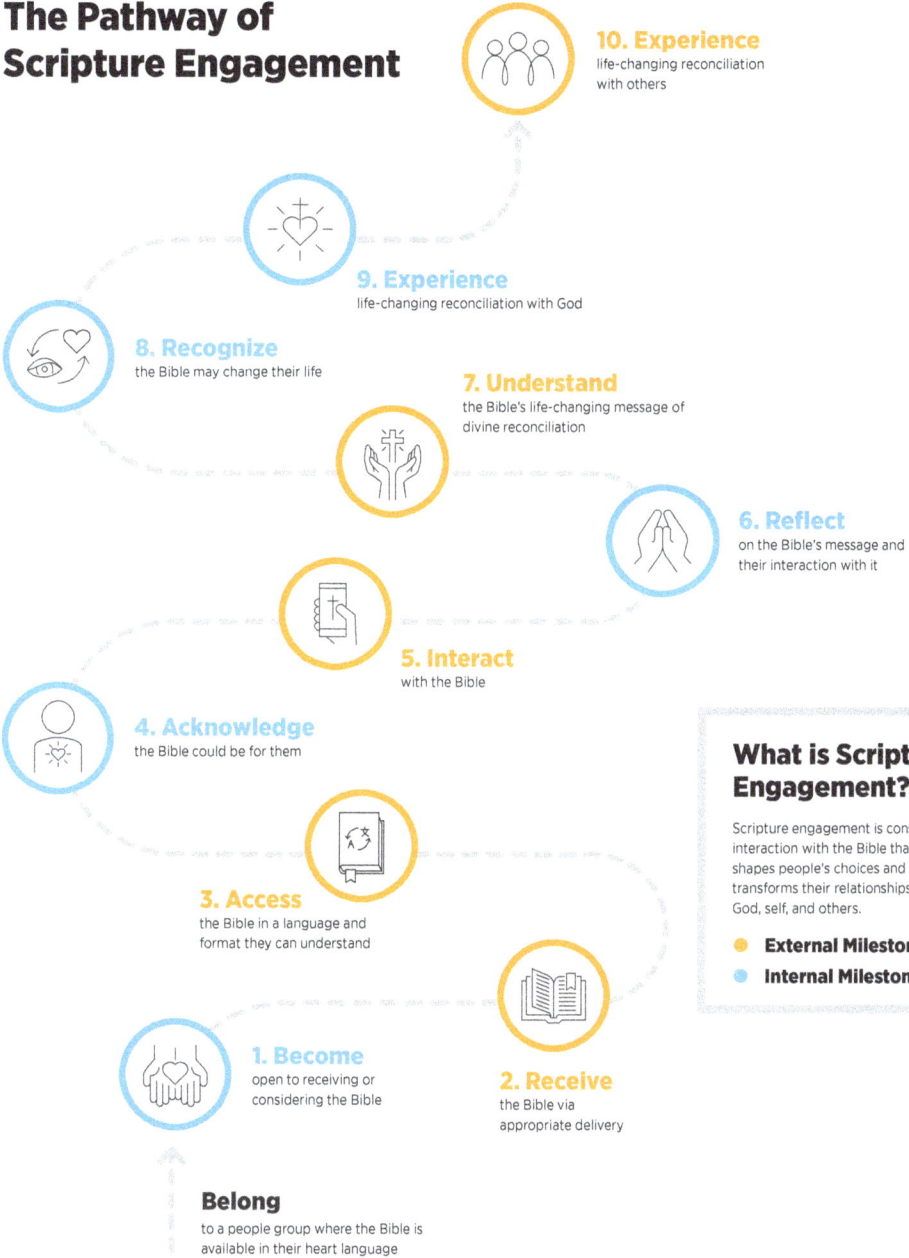

10. Experience
life-changing reconciliation with others

9. Experience
life-changing reconciliation with God

8. Recognize
the Bible may change their life

7. Understand
the Bible's life-changing message of divine reconciliation

6. Reflect
on the Bible's message and their interaction with it

5. Interact
with the Bible

4. Acknowledge
the Bible could be for them

3. Access
the Bible in a language and format they can understand

1. Become
open to receiving or considering the Bible

2. Receive
the Bible via appropriate delivery

Belong
to a people group where the Bible is available in their heart language

What is Scripture Engagement?

Scripture engagement is consistent interaction with the Bible that shapes people's choices and transforms their relationships with God, self, and others.

- ● **External Milestone**
- ● **Internal Milestone**

those tasks, we use the Scripture Engagement Survey to locate an individual on the Scripture Engagement Scale (SES).

The SES is designed to plot an individual's current location on the Pathway and—with repeated measurement—their progress (growth) toward spiritual health. Using a brief survey, individuals and groups can be located on the Pathway[1] and matched to transformative, Bible-based ministry interventions that catalyze movement toward spiritual health.

By translating the Pathway's basic map into an accurate GPS, the Scripture Engagement Scale can guide individuals to the next step in their spiritual journey. It can also help ministry leaders design and deploy discipleship tools that are appropriate to people at every stage of the spiritual formation journey.

---

1 Based on our research, a score of 100 on the Scripture Engagement Scale corresponds approximately to step 6 on the Pathway of Scripture Engagement.

ACKNOWLEDGMENTS

Since 2011, American Bible Society has sponsored the annual *State of the Bible* research study in an effort to listen carefully to America's voice regarding the Bible, faith, and the church. Today, the science of listening is a main focus of the Insights & Innovation team at American Bible Society.

This book is the effort of a small army of gifted individuals who combine their skills and perspectives to produce what you hold in your hand or view on your screen. In this fifteenth consecutive year of the *State of the Bible*, we pause to express our gratitude to those who have contributed most to this work.

The *State of the Bible* research team is led by American Bible Society's Chief Innovation Officer, Dr. John Plake, who joined the team for the 2018 study. Since that time, Dr. Plake has helped to expand American Bible Society's research capabilities, making it possible for us to lead the *State of the Bible* research and produce this report. Dr. Plake serves as the editor-in-chief of this report and oversees the ongoing *State of the Bible* series.

Dr. Jeff Fulks serves as Senior Research Fellow, where he brings deep insight from the world of behavioral science research and serves as the lead analyst for the *State of the Bible* research. He skillfully incorporates research-proven measures into our work, and leverages years of research experience to uncover the story behind the numbers.

Sandra Siggins serves as Research and Evaluation Manager, performing countless statistical tests and preparing reams of data for our writing and data visualization specialists. She coordinates interviews with our subject matter experts and helps keep the reporting organized and on schedule.

Randy Petersen of Petersen Creative Enterprises serves as *State of the Bible's* managing editor and lead writer. Randy served for nearly four years as American Bible Society's Director of Scripture Engagement Content. During his tenure at ABS, Randy helped the team write about research and data. He has a gift for parsimony: bringing clarity to complexity without sacrificing truth.

Josh Thomassen of Thomassen Collective handles data visualizations, graphic design, and typesetting. He joined the *State of the Bible* team in 2023 and is bringing a fresh look to our data visualizations and graphics.

Peter Edman is our editorial and quality assurance lead, helping all of us produce a more consistent, high-quality report. We also have regular input from Elisabeth Trefsgar and Bran Van Deinse in assuring sensitivity to the many SOTB audiences.

www.ingramcontent.com/pod-product-compliance
Lightning Source LLC
Chambersburg PA
CBHW040832300326
R18048400001B/R180484PG41927CBX00013B/1